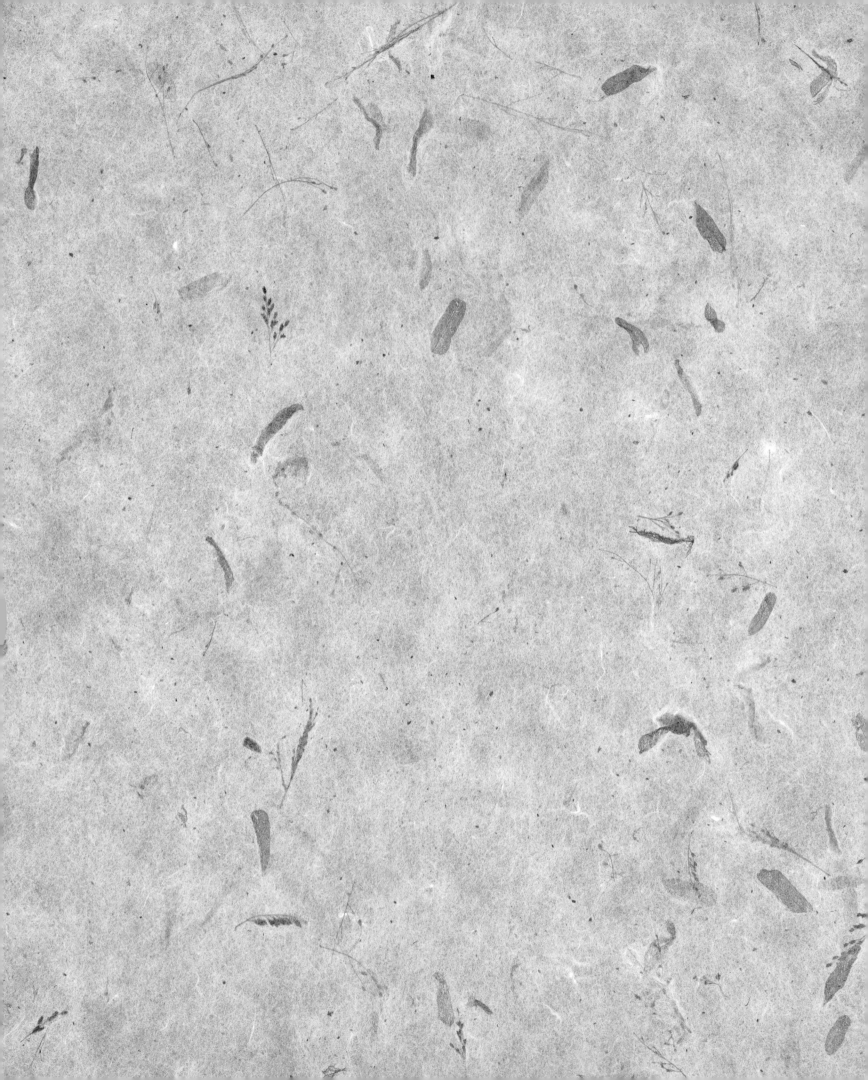

NORTHERN TREASURE

NORTHERN TREASURE

THE MINNESOTA LANDSCAPE ARBORETUM AND HORTICULTURAL RESEARCH CENTER

University of Minnesota

TEXT BY SUSAN DAVIS PRICE

PHOTOGRAPHS BY JOHN GREGOR

afton press

The publication of

NORTHERN TREASURE

THE MINNESOTA LANDSCAPE ARBORETUM AND HORTICULTURAL RESEARCH CENTER

has been made possible by generous gifts from

Nivin S. MacMillan and the WDM Foundation

Leland and Louise Sundet

and

The Scrooby Foundation

Hella and Bill Hueg

Roger and Nancy McCabe

Louise (Rusty) H. Huff

Martha Beam de Vos

Front cover: Crabapple Collection. Photograph by John Gregor.
p. 2 (opposite half-title): Iris Garden with waterfall. Photograph by John Gregor.
Frontispiece: Rainbow view over Linden Collection. Photograph by John Gregor.
Back cover: Red Barn over hedges. Photograph by Floyd L. Goodwyn, III.

Except as noted below, the photographs in **NORTHERN TREASURE** *are the work of photographer John Gregor.*

JULIE BROPHY
p. 106, group of hikers

GREG HARTWELL
p. 132, "Big Bug"

NIVIN MACMILLAN
p. 7, Duncan MacMillan

MINNESOTA LANDSCAPE ARBORETUM
p. 28; p. 29, Peter Gideon; p. 31, processing fruit; p. 32, Charles Haralson; p. 33, truck; p. 34, Fred Haralson; p. 35 (top), Fruit Breeding Farm; p. 35 (bottom), Fruit Farm; p. 36, Professors Leon C. Snyder and T. H. Weir; p. 40, Dr. Harold Pellett; p. 44, tractor; p. 48-49, Arboretum buildings; p. 51, Dr. Leon C. Snyder; p. 52, Dr. Francis de Vos; p. 96, map; p. 107, ground-breaking of the Snyder Education Building; p. 108, tour group; p. 120, Dave Bedford, p. 125-126, Library; p. 130, The Fall Festival

MELISSA SCHMITT
p. 38, Red Barn; p. 55, Secret Gardens

Edited by Marcia Aubineau
Designed by Mary Susan Oleson
Production assistance by Beth Williams
Printed by Pettit Network Inc., Afton, Minnesota

Library of Congress Cataloging-in-Publication Data
Price, Susan Davis.
Northern treasure / by Susan Davis Price.—1st ed.
    p. cm.
ISBN 978-1-890434-77-9 (hardcover: alk. paper)
1. University of Minnesota. Landscape Arboretum—History. I.Title.

QK480.M62U556 2008
580.73'77653--dc22

                                        2008000975

Printed in China

Paul A. Verret
PRESIDENT

Patricia Condon McDonald
PUBLISHER

AFTON HISTORICAL SOCIETY PRESS
P.O. Box 100, Afton, MN 55001
800-436-8443
aftonpress@aftonpress.com
www.aftonpress.com

REMEMBERING

W. Duncan MacMillan
(1930-2006)

who encouraged
and supported
the best in
horticulture,
history, and books

CONTENTS

FOREWORD by Peter Olin   10

1 SEASONS   12

2 HISTORY   28

3 BUILDING   42

4 GARDENS   56

5 DEPARTMENTS and PROGRAMS   104

APPENDIX   135
NOTES   136
ACKNOWLEDGMENTS   137
INDEX   138

IN THE GRAND SCHEME of things, fifty years is not a great time span. However, all time is relative. If you're fifteen, fifty years is ancient history; if you're fifty, it's mid-life; and if you're well beyond fifty, it's just yesterday! Age, however, is important to an institution. There is "young" when it has just begun, then there is "been here for a while," and finally an institution moves to "established." I like to think of the Minnesota Landscape Arboretum as "established."

When Leon Snyder was cajoled into starting an arboretum to test woody plants for Minnesota's climate, he probably looked to the Arnold Arboretum, a prestigious institution attached to Harvard University. The Arnold is one of the most famous research gardens in the country, where collected species were planted and observed, and their reaction to the environment recorded. Leon created an Arnold Arboretum west, a northern research arboretum, and it became, during his tenure, the northern United States testing ground for plant hardiness.

When Leon retired and Francis de Vos took over, de Vos also looked to the Arnold Arboretum, but he realized that like the Arnold, the university he was affiliated with was not going to support a long-term effort to maintain plant collections. So de Vos looked more closely at the public garden he had directed in Chicago, the Chicago Botanic Garden, as a model. He then began to change the Minnesota Landscape Arboretum into a public garden, a regional and national destination of outstanding beauty. This is not to say the research and plant collections were abandoned, but

they were certainly superseded as de Vos took advantage of the spectacular site, introducing a beautifully designed rose garden, demonstration gardens for home owners, many smaller gardens, and a beautiful perennial garden as a centerpiece. These changes were to place the Landscape Arboretum into the forefront of public gardens, but de Vos's concept was not totally accepted by Arboretum supporters.

Arriving at the Arboretum as interim director before Francis retired and then being hired as Director, I found a wide range of thought about our future. I had some knowledge of horticulture, landscape architecture, teaching and some life experience, but it took several years for me to understand the Arboretum, its importance, just exactly what had taken place, and finally where this institution should be headed. On a steep learning curve, I observed what was happening around the country and what role public gardens were playing in society, how they accomplished the job and mostly how they funded their work. My time has been spent setting direction, building the operational base, funding it, and adding the programs that I hope most support our societal role and responsibility. Again, a direction not totally accepted by all Arboretum visitors.

One could easily ask, just what is the role of an arboretum or botanic garden in today's society? I use the terms arboretum, botanic garden, and public garden somewhat interchangeably, but the importance of such institutions became loud and clear to me. They are responsible for the necessary work of understanding and preserving plants as the basis of life on earth and bringing that understanding to the public.

Each year the earth loses many species of plants, plants we hardly know. The only active organizations looking at saving plants are a few universities and many public gardens. The goal today is to save plants *in situ* (i.e. in the place where they grow naturally). To accomplish this requires a huge educational, regulatory and promotional effort on the part of public gardens. It also means that if this cannot be accomplished, we must save the plants *ex situ* at our garden sites. The Minnesota Landscape Arboretum is involved in maintaining extensive native areas to preserve native Minnesota flora but also with efforts to aid northern gardens in other parts of the world in saving their indigenous flora.

Educating the local populace about the importance of plants in our everyday life has been relegated in many ways to botanic gardens and arboreta. Our nation's elementary and secondary schools barely touch upon plant science, botany departments at universities have disappeared, and public gardens have been left to pick up the slack. Most gardens, including the MLA, concentrate on educating children because they are receptive, and sound environmental principles can be instilled early on.

To reach adults with solid environmental information, the MLA presents facts so that people may make up their own minds, especially when it concerns their personal environments of work, play and home. Information sheets, interpretive signage, web sites and best of all, models to be experienced by the visitor, make the MLA an excellent place to educate adults. We present learning opportunities in informal, non-threatening, fun ways in a beautiful setting. This is undoubtedly the most important job that public gardens accomplish in terms of affecting the environmental quality of the everyday lives of our citizens.

Often discounted, even by botanic gardens and arboreta themselves, however, is the critical aspect of giving our visitors a meaningful, quality experience. Individuals can benefit physically through recreational and exercise-oriented activities, spiritually by communing with nature and all that that might imply, socially by engaging in great conversations with friends or by volunteering, and emotionally by reorienting their outlook and feelings and recharging their spirits. These are not minor matters that imply icing on the cake; these are the attitudinal changes that send people forth with a new outlook. This is the "stuff of life" which becomes more important every year as our lives and our society become more complex and consequently more difficult to navigate.

In the end, a botanical refuge like the Minnesota Landscape Arboretum is one of the few places that works to give us environmental stability, as well as opportunities to gain solace, to learn, to recreate, and to enjoy. In this book we explore what the Arboretum is about and where we have come from, and hopefully give the reader some idea of where we are headed. Our vision is clear, our mission strong, and our commitment intense. We are here for you—our friends, our members, our casual visitors—and we are here for the future well-being of the people of Minnesota and of the world. I think all of our Arboretum friends would agree to this!

PETER OLIN, DIRECTOR, MINNESOTA LANDSCAPE ARBORETUM
AND HORTICULTURAL RESEARCH CENTER

SEASONS

CHAPTER ONE

THE FIRST OF MARCH may not feel like spring in Minnesota. Snow covers the ground and arctic blasts may still whip across the plains. But those who look and listen closely will find sure signs of the change in seasons.

One of the first spring sounds is the drip, drip, dripping of sap from taps in the sugar maples. Usually the Arboretum starts tapping trees, nearly two hundred of them, during the first week of March. By then, with daytime temperatures rising above forty degrees and nights still dropping below freezing, sap flow is at its peak. Staff and volunteers assist with the tapping, their efforts culminating in the Sugarbush Pancake Brunch, an annual event since 1986, featuring the Arboretum's own maple syrup.

Another sound that signals the arrival of spring is the soprano whistle of the black-capped chickadees. And as the days pass, the feathered chorale adds altos and basses: the drumming of the red-bellied woodpeckers and the deep-pitched *hoo, hoo-oo, hoo, hoo* of the great horned owls. Soon the melting snow brings in more singers—early migrant red-wing black birds, killdeer, and American robins—as their audience, gophers and chipmunks just out of winter retirement, scurries by below the trees.

By late March, the delicate snow-drops (*Galanthus*)

Tulip Tarda is one of the early bloomers in the Arboretum's rock garden.

with their white, bell-like flowers, are in blossom, and soon the pink and lavender blooms of the sharp-lobed hepaticas (*Hepatica acutiloba*) will be popping up on the maple-basswood forest floor.

April brings milder weather and more signs of spring. The pristine white bloodroot (*Sanguinaria canadensis*) blankets the woods, accompanied by the rare, pale pink Minnesota trout lily (*Erythronium propullans*). As trees begin to bud, a variety of ferns and other woodland flowers carpet the Arboretum's forest floor with the subtle hues of the season.

In the Arboretum's gardens, scilla and crocus burst forth in a riot of color, followed in turn by masses of tulips, daffodils, and hyacinths. Pansies, thousands of them, greet visitors at the entrance on Alkire Drive, the new green leaves of the trees forming a brilliant backdrop to the blossoms.

By this time, the ice is out on Green Heron Pond, spring peepers are vocalizing, and painted turtles are sunning themselves. Migrating mergansers can be spotted on the small pond in the Grace B. Dayton Wildflower Garden.

Vibrant masses of cheerful daffodils add splashes of color to the spring landscape.

In the Palma J. Wilson Rose Garden, Minnesota Rose Society members are engaged in unearthing more than two hundred plants that have been buried since October. For more than twenty-five years, Rose Society members have helped maintain this site, providing funds for plants and fertilizer, assisting with deadheading the spent blossoms, and preparing the roses for winter. Later this month, they will conduct demonstrations on correct rose pruning for growers from throughout the region.

Out on the open prairie, the warmth of May brings forth pasque flowers (*Pulsatilla patens*), prairie smoke (*Geum triflorum*), and golden Alexanders (*Zizia aurea*). In the swamps and lowlands, the splashy yellow marsh marigolds (*Caltha palustris*) and the tan-brown hoods of the skunk cabbage (*Symplocarpus foetidus*) appear. Along the rock garden slopes, mat-forming plants—rock cress, aubrietia and phlox—color the ground with their blossoms. Rhododendrons and then azaleas, many of them the Arboretum's own introductions, paint the hillsides with pink and rose, gold and peach, while the air is filled with the enchanting fragrance of dozens of large lilacs along the Staples Lilac Walk.

As spring progresses, crabapples burst forth into blossom throughout the Arboretum.

Through its history, the Horticultural Research Center has worked to hybridize numerous edible and ornamental plants, perhaps most famously and consistently the apple, and by May, the hillsides along Highway 5 are lit with the soft colors of blossoms portending the autumn crops of 'Sweet Sixteen,' 'Regent,' Honeycrisp™, 'Fireside,' 'Beacon,' Zestar!™,

Spring Plant Sale. Initially the sale's offerings consisted of divisions of plants found within the MLA itself. So, when the peonies needed dividing, they were potted up and made available to the public. The sale has long outgrown this practice and at present also handles plant stock bought from wholesalers. In 1970 the volunteers of the Arboretum Auxiliary took over the handling of the

In the Hueg Lilac Collection, hundreds of bushes fill the air with soft colors and sweet fragrance.

and Minnesota's favorite, the 'Haralson.' And tucked into the branches of these trees, a crop of another sort is being prepared for as the gray and white eastern kingbirds ready their nests for a new brood.

Since the early years of the Minnesota Landscape Arboretum, this has also been the season of the annual

sale. When they met on the third of June, one week after it was over, to tally the results, they were amazed to see they had grossed $7,200—$5,000 of which was profit. By 2004, the group was bringing in eighteen times that amount and its profits were up 700 percent! What originally had been a one-day sale has become a three-day affair where thousands of plants of all kinds, from annuals to trees, are sold to an eager public.

As the sun shifts its arc and spring gives way to summer, the Arboretum's lighter pastel palette of April and May gives way to the subtle blues and pinks of June, eventually succumbing to the deep yellows and oranges of August. The perennial gardens—the Richard

In July the Burke Griggs Annual Garden is the place to be. Each year, landscape gardener Duane Otto chooses a color theme for the Arboretum. That theme, be it primary colors, royal reds and purples, or variations of citrus, casts its influence in all the annual plantings. The containers, walkways, hanging baskets, and the Highway 5 entrance garden are planted in similar tones, but

The Palma J. Wilson Rose Garden with its heady perfume and velvety colors invites visitors to linger.

and Judith Spiegel Entrance Garden, the Sarah Stevens MacMillan Terrace Garden, and the Elizabeth Carr Slade Perennial Garden—beckon with masses of blossoms all season long. June's floral regent is the iris. By the Iris Pond, tall bearded iris flower during the first two weeks of the month, eventually followed by the beardless varieties.

the most lavish expression is visible in the Burke Griggs Annual Garden itself. Here the classical lines of stone walls and paths are softened by the blossoms of over 7,500 colorful plants.

By late summer the Bennett/Johnson Prairie has grown tall and is splattered with bright summer hues. The blossoms of the aster, sky blue (*Aster azureus*) and smooth (*A. laevis*), nod in the breeze. Tall compass and cup plants (*Silphium laciniatum* and *perfoliatum*) reach their yellow heads to the sky, and big bluestem (*Andropogon gerardi*) and Indian grass (*Sorghastrum nutans*) display dangling golden anthers. Anyone taking in the visual beauty of the scene will also be soothed by the whish of the grasses in the wind, the dickcissel singing out its name (*dick dick ciss ciss ciss*), and the cheerful warbling of the bobolink.

vide the visitor with a sensual feast. There are aromas, textures, shapes, and blossoms to admire, and the winding path through the Fragrant Garden allows visitors easy access to the plants.

Summer months are filled with work as well, as staff and volunteers swarm over the gardens. Many volunteers have worked here loyally for years, some several days a week, planting annuals, filling baskets, weeding,

One of six herb gardens at the Arboretum, the Fragrant Garden is at its best in the warm months.

Those wishing for a cool spot on a hot day can do no better than the Pauline Whitney MacMillan Hosta Glade. In the garden the overhanging trees filter out the harsh sunlight, and the many green leaves absorb the heat.

The warm months also bring out the best in herbs. A stroll through any of the six herb gardens is sure to pro-

and deadheading. Without their help, the Arboretum would be a much less colorful place.

Down in the Children's Garden, youngsters aged eight to thirteen are busy preparing soil and planting seeds. Since 1975, urban and suburban children have taken part in this summer-long introduction to gardening.

The Bennett/Johnson Prairie is a colorful reminder of Minnesota's
earlier landscape. Here coneflowers and grasses stand tall.

Peonies of all colors line the Lang Peony Walk.

Here they plant and tend vegetables and fruit, not only learning gardening skills and plant identification, but also cooperation and team work. During an early August weekend, participants welcome everyone to the garden for the annual Children's Harvest Fair.

All summer, activities for families and individuals abound. Thursdays, after 4:30 P.M., admission to the Arboretum is free. Every Thursday night there are family-oriented cultural and horticultural programs. Arboretum staff and docents lead visitors on a variety of tours to explore the prairie, woodlands, bogs, and sedge meadows. On these tours visitors are able to wander off the beaten track and discover the Arboretum's more hidden corners.

Since 2003 a themed exhibition has also been featured every summer. Its interactive exhibits, featured throughout the gardens, are designed to interest all

"Secret Gardens" was the theme for interactive exhibits throughout the Arboretum in the summer of 2006. This "secret garden" flourished in front of the Oswald Visitor Center.

ages. Themes have included "Wild about Birds," "Secret Gardens," and "Amazing Mazes."

In August, as a thank-you to its members, the Arboretum hosts an evening of old-fashioned fun with an ice cream social. In addition to the ice cream, this popular event features music, balloons, garden tours, and activities for both children and adults, and every year attendance grows.

In September the crisp days of autumn replace summer's heat, and the gardens, perennial and annual, prosper as the season's rains and cooler temperatures give the plants new vigor. Fall bloomers—chrysanthemums, asters, Japanese anemone (*Anemone hupehensis*), and turtle head (*Chelone*)—add color to the perennial beds. The roses in the Wilson Rose Garden get a fresh start with the cool fall temperatures, and the flowers in the Dahlia Test Garden have never looked better.

The boardwalk in Spring Peeper Meadow affords a fine view of the marsh and its wildlife. The small, sunflower-like heads of nodding beggar's-ticks (*Bidens cernua*) and frothy-white Boltonia (*Boltonia asteroides*) brighten up the water's edge. Nearby, the brilliant blue bottle gentian (*Gentiana andrewsii*) shines out among the red and gold of the grasses. From the Gallistel Overlook, visitors can take in the entire scene—forest, prairie, and marsh—and thus catch a glimpse of the Minnesota landscape that greeted the first European arrivals.

At the end of August the Apple House opens, offering fruit grown on the Horticultural Research Center grounds. The sale opens with Zestar!™, followed by 'Red Baron' and 'Chestnut Crab.' Evaluators have consistently rated the recent introduction Zestar!™ a favorite among the "earlies." Crisp and juicy, its flavor is slightly more sweet than tart. By late September, 'Red Haralson,' 'Haralson,' Honeycrisp™, 'Prairie Spy,' and 'Cortland' are available. In October, the richly flavored

A stalwart Arboretum sugar maple in autumn garb.

'Fireside,' 'Connell Red,' and the sweet/tart 'Regent' round out the season.

On Sunday, September 29, 1968, the first Autumn Festival, as it was then called, was held. It was initiated by a committee of ten women, volunteer tour guides, who thought an autumn fund-raising event was a good idea for the ten-year-old Arboretum.

The day included sales of homemade goodies, activities and demonstrations, a raffle, and an auction. The machine shed, later called Frog Hollow after its location, became the General Store; the Ordway Shelter was called the School House. There were apple and candy

With the Apple House in full swing, school groups make field trips to sample a taste of fall.

NORTHERN TREASURE

The Grace B. Dayton Wildflower Garden awash in autumn color.

stands, and lunch was served. Festival-goers toured the grounds in a tractor-pulled hay rack.

The committee had hoped to attract two thousand people. In fact, many more showed up, so many that by ten o'clock in the morning, Arboretum organizers had called in the help of the Carver County Mounted Posse for crowd control. Within the first hour, all the jams, jellies, and baked goods were gone. By the day's end, volunteers had made a profit of $2,500 and a new event had been inaugurated, one which has continued to be wildly successful for over thirty-eight years.

As the leaves turn, the forested areas are lit up with russets and yellows and scarlets, magnificent against the blue October sky. A hike along Three-Mile Drive or through the Grace B. Dayton Wildflower Garden provides visitors an opportunity to enjoy the Arboretum with its woods aglow. Those wanting a more leisurely trip can take the Trumpet Creeper Tram for a one-hour seasonal tour.

Amateur and professional photographers have recognized the Arboretum's autumnal beauty and arrive to claim their favorite spots and try their hand at capturing what Keats referred to in his ode "To Autumn" as that "season of mists and mellow fruitfulness, / Close bosom-friend of the maturing sun." Staff members have their favorite nooks and crannies too. Director of Operations Peter Moe recommends standing in the woods by the Berens Cabin when the sun streams down through the leaves, and long-time volunteer Helen King suggests sitting on the hill in the prairie to take in the view.

In the Slade Perennial Garden, the bold colors of autumn call out for attention.

Mists over Green Heron Pond accentuate the mysterious beauty of autumn.

Since 1990, early in October the Friends of the Andersen Horticultural Library have arrived to hold their annual used book sale. Numerous volunteers sort, arrange, and sell over twenty thousand used books. Although many of the titles are garden-related, the selections cover a world of fiction and non-fiction. The healthy proceeds benefit the library's book and periodical budgets, supplement its equipment needs, and add to its endowment.

As the snows and cold of winter put the gardens to bed, the Arboretum's beauty is changed but not diminished. Now instead of colorful dahlias and maple trees, there are new silhouettes and shapes to admire. Visitors can appreciate the contours of the hillocks and

ravines, the ponds and rivulets, the branches of conifers, or patches of snow along the stone walls. Three-Mile Drive is available for hiking, and visitors can snowshoe across the tranquil prairie or cross-country ski on one of the groomed trails that wind through the pristine beauty of the landscape.

Alert observers will see a variety of wildlife. Cardinals—splashes of crimson against the blanched landscape—frequent the birdfeeders, as do black-capped chickadees, tree sparrows, juncos, and wild turkeys. The feeders also attract red and gray squirrels, short-tailed weasels, and white-tailed deer. In the open field at the Horticultural Research Center, the ground-loving snow buntings find shelter beneath a solitary tuft of

This female cardinal, puffed up in winter, has probably been feasting on the Arboretum's bounty of berries and seeds.

foxes, jackrabbits, muskrats, mink, and raccoons all claim the MLA as their winter habitat.

In the gardens, frost-covered seed heads sparkle in the morning light, and grasses, covered in ice, bend in the wind. With the first snow fall, the conifers are transformed into stately white sculptures. The colorful barks of trees stand out against the white backdrop—the dark bark of Russian olive, the metallic covering of the Amur chokecherry—and the fruits of mountain ash, highbush cranberries, Korean barberry, and flowering crabapples add brilliant color to the landscape.

The Japanese feel that snow adds "winter flowers" to the evergreens and the bare branches of deciduous trees and shrubs. What better place to observe this phenomenon than in the Japanese Garden, Seisui-Tei, where the pines and ginnala maples catch the snow and transform it into hoary statues.

dried grass, a leafless bush, or a burrow of soft snow. In flight, a flock looks like a whirling flurry of wind-whipped snow flakes.

Red-tailed hawks will usually return each year to the same patch of woods to nest. Recently, they have been known to raise their young in the Berens Woods along the North Star Walking Trail. In mild seasons they will overwinter there. These large birds can often be seen soaring in great circles above the Arboretum, and beneath their arcs, tracks in the snow give evidence that other animals are on the grounds as well. Red and gray

Those who like to appreciate winter from the inside will also find much to enjoy. The restaurant offers up tea and muffins as well as full meals along with the opportunity to observe the season's wonders through a long wall of windows. Outside, the Oswald Visitor Center terraces are bedecked with arrangements of fruit, form, and texture.

In the Andersen Horticultural Library gardeners can get inspiration for next year's plots from hundreds of gardening texts. After designing or redoing their personal landscape plans, they can also discover which nurseries and seed houses carry the plants they've chosen. Friendly and knowledgeable members of the library staff are on hand to help.

NORTHERN TREASURE

Silhouetted in the snow: sculptor Paul Granlund's *Winter and Summer Nymphs*.

HISTORY

IN THE EARLY DAYS of its settlement, Minnesota was viewed as a frigid region with doubtful agricultural possibilities. The eastern pundit, Horace Greeley, who urged young men to go west, advised against heading to Minnesota. The reason, he said: "They can't grow apples there!"

True enough, there were few fruits found growing here naturally, and with the exception of some plums, all were of inferior quality. Never ones to ignore a challenge, however, the early pioneers set about to develop homegrown, delicious foods for their tables and larders. Unfortunately, their efforts were rarely successful.

Farmers like John Harris, Reverend G. H. Pond, and Swedish immigrant Andrew Peterson (whose forty-year diary served as a source of information for Vilhelm Moberg's novels—*The Emigrants, Unto a Good Land,* and *The Last Letter Home*—worked in relative obscurity to find varieties with improved taste as well as the increased hardiness necessary to withstand both Minnesota's brutal Januarys and torrid Julys. One account in *The History of Free-*

born County describes the futile efforts of Isaac W. McReynolds, who had planted apple seeds in 1858:

However, like most of the early seedling orchards that were grown from promiscuous seed gathered from eastern orchards, they carried with them in their ancestry *no special adaptation to the climate of the West,* [emphasis added] and one by one they succumbed to severe winters and droughty summers, till at the end of twenty years very little was left to show for the effort that had been put forth.[1]

Most persistent of all these early farmers, perhaps, and certainly the most eccentric, was Peter Miller Gideon. Born in Ohio in 1820, Gideon came to Lake Minnetonka in 1853 bearing a bushel of apple seed and an unshakeable faith in his ability to grow fruit. There he homesteaded on the side of the bay which now carries his name.

Peter Gideon arrived at Lake Minnetonka in 1853 and worked for over ten years to develop an apple hardy enough to survive a Minnesota winter. In 1868 he produced the tasty and attractive 'Wealthy,' named for his wife.

Gideon began by planting thirty named varieties of apples and a good collection of other fruits, but although he added to his orchard annually, by the tenth year every tree except one seedling crab had fallen victim to the severe Minnesota winters. With only one cow and fewer than twenty chickens to his name, and a wife and children to feed, Gideon was desperate. He took a deep breath, sent his last eight dollars to Maine for seeds and scion wood (grafting material), and waited for spring in a home-made jacket he had sewn from two old vests—a winter suit "more odd than ornamental" by his own account.[2]

In his *History of Horticulture in America to 1860*, U. P. Hedrick states that Gideon "was the only man in America to pay attention to apple breeding before 1860,"[3] and his persistence was rewarded on receiving from Maine seeds of the 'Duchess,' 'Blue Pearmain,' and 'Cherry' crab. He then crossed the larger varieties with the hardy crabapple, and the result, in 1868, was the 'Wealthy' (named in honor of his wife)—a good-looking, tasty fruit that would survive the region's winters.

Still grown locally, the 'Wealthy'—which is full-sized, bears regularly, and has reasonable keeping qualities— became immensely popular. Its success led directly to the Minnesota Legislature's approval of state-supported experimentation in fruit breeding. In March 1878, at the urging of the Minnesota State Horticultural Society, the legislature established the "Minnetonka Fruit Farm" on a 116-acre plot next to Gideon's land. Gideon himself was appointed superintendent and the farm was placed under the jurisdiction of the University of Minnesota.

For twelve years Gideon supervised the Fruit Farm, continuing apple experimentation, particularly the development of "long keepers," but introducing no new varieties during that time. When he retired in 1889, the land was sold. Gideon's eccentric nature and his determination to operate as a lone wolf probably contributed to the Farm's demise, but his work there encouraged later botanical developments. For example, in 1883 the Minnesota State Horticulture Society established a series of experiment stations for testing ornamentals and vegetables as well as fruit. The results of their experiments were published twice a year in the *Minnesota Horticulturist*.

In 1907 the State Horticultural Society lobbied the legislature for a fruit breeding and testing farm to be a part of the University of Minnesota's Horticulture Department. In its report, the Society said, "Such a farm is greatly needed to place the state's horticultural work in a satisfactory condition."[4] Further, they stated that the $16,000 gained from selling the Minnetonka Fruit Farm could be used to purchase new acreage. Their request was approved the same year, and a seventy-eight-acre tract five miles west of Excelsior was purchased from Daniel Fink. Additional acreage was purchased in 1920 and 1931, bringing the total to approximately 230 acres.

The Fruit Breeding Farm was reached easily by train from Minneapolis and the University of Minnesota's St. Paul campus. Describing the tract, the Horticultural Society noted, "It is located in what is called the 'big woods' region, soil growing naturally hard maple and basswood, though this farm has been under cultivation long enough so that the fields are entirely free from stumps and roots. The land has been well cared for and its fertility kept up."[5]

The Farm was incorporated as part of the University's Department of Horticulture and Charles Haralson was named as first superintendent. In taking the job, Haralson sounded a note that has been echoed through the decades: "We are near the northern limits of fruit growing and therefore must grow seedlings from our hardiest varieties to secure the best results."[6] Haralson, formerly of South Dakota State College, held the position of superintendent until 1923, and his longevity at the Farm contributed to its successes.

In 1908 a greenhouse was constructed and the real work of plant breeding began. Haralson, as have many breeders since, recommended looking at the region's

In 1914, processing fruit at the Fruit Farm was a very labor-intensive undertaking.

native wild fruits as well as cultivated ones. Surplus nursery stock from the Central Experiment Station and donations by local farmers and fruit growers—including 'Malinda' apples, 'Beta' grapes, raspberries, plums and strawberries—were the first plants installed.

By 1912, sixty-five acres were under intensive cultivation, low places had been drained, and needed buildings constructed. Many fruits were sent out to Horticultural Society members for trial, the first (in 1914) being the Minnesota No. 4 red raspberry, later named 'Latham.' Two years later, when Haralson

Charles Haralson, superintendent of the Fruit Farm, developed the 'Haralson' apple, still a favorite with Minnesotans.

summarized his fruit breeding efforts, he noted work on apples, cherries, grapes, pears, and raspberries, also reporting that the greatest success had come with strawberries—an ever-bearing and a June-bearing strain showing most promise.

The winter of 1917-18, a "test" winter, was unusually severe, and apples died at a greater rate than during any season previously, yet there were survivors, most importantly the progeny of 'Malinda,' originally from New England. These survivors led to successful apple releases in the 1920s, the 'Haralson' and 'Beacon,' and became the basis for Minnesota apple breeding up through the present time. By 1923, twenty-nine new varieties of fruits and ornamentals had joined the still wildly popular 'Latham' raspberry. The large number of introductions in such a short period of time showed what great progress had been made in the Minnesota fruit growing industry.[7]

In 1923, Professor W. H. Alderman, head of the University's Horticulture Department, took over as superintendent, living and working at the Farm during the three summer months when he was not teaching in St. Paul. Alderman appointed Fred Haralson, a brother of Charles, as his assistant. Haralson, who was there year-round and in charge of all the breeding efforts, served as assistant superintendent until his retirement in 1946 when Professor T. H. Weir took his position.

Regardless of the Farm's achievements, however, year after year, the superintendent and the examining committee from the Minnesota Horticulture Society were faced with the problem of insufficient funding. In 1918

Shown here in 1919, a truck was used to deliver Fruit Farm apples.

the committee noted that Charles Haralson found it necessary to perform much of the manual labor himself, reducing the time he was able to devote to scientific work. In 1925 the committee reported that the greenhouses, in which much of the breeding work was done, were closed down for the winter due to a lack of coal.

Various measures were initiated to address the problem. For example, during the Depression years, the WPA (Works Progress Administration) provided labor for several major projects. Beginning in 1938 the Farm cooperated with the U.S. Department of Agriculture in the National Fruit Breeding Program. As part of this agreement, the federal agency provided funds of $1,000 a year to pay for the part-time employment of USDA field agents to assist in fruit breeding.

Another perennial concern was the weather. In 1916 Charles Haralson stated in his report, "As is known to all of us, the past summer was one of unusual severity on all kinds of fruit."[8] The spring had been "very wet and backward,"[9] followed by the most severe drought on record. Likewise, in 1929, Fred Haralson wrote of the previous year, "Like most seasons, that of 1928 was somewhat unusual."[10] He reported that spring conditions had caused late bloom, and most difficult of all,

. . . early in August the worst storm in the history of the Fruit Breeding Farm swept thru the western Minnetonka areas. It blew off or injured practically all of the apples that had been set, removed one-half of the plum crop, and bruised so many that remained that brown rot promptly set in with very destructive results. The raspberry crop was shortened by 3 pickings. The destruction of trees and property by the wind was also considerable.[11]

In 1934 the annual report noted that "the most discouraging feature of the past season's experiences was the unusually severe and prolonged drought which covered both the dormant and the growing season."[12]

However, despite budget restraints and difficult weather, breeders at the Farm continued to make significant progress. Under superintendent Alderman and Fred Haralson, a large variety of fruits, wild and cultivated, were studied and many crosses made. The Farm's policy was to not introduce any fruit that was not a distinct improvement over an earlier one.

Fred Haralson, brother of Charles, was assistant superintendent of the Fruit Farm from 1923 to 1946.

Between 1919 and 1953, sixty-two fruit and three ornamental varieties were named and presented to the public. Besides the 'Haralson' and 'Beacon' apples and the 'Latham' raspberry, notable introductions included the 'Fireside' apple, 'Chestnut' crab, 'Meteor' and 'North Star' cherries, 'Red Lake' currant, and 'Superior' plum.

The Farm's work benefited both individual growers and commercial ones. According to a report in the 1934 *Minnesota Horticulturist*, the red raspberry industry of Minnesota ranked first among all states east of the Rocky Mountains. The 'Latham' raspberry had brought in more money than the entire cost of the Farm and all maintenance to that date, and the 'Haralson' apple was said to generate more income per tree than any other apple raised in the state. (By 2005, the 'Haralson' represented 50 percent of Minnesota's apple production.) As a 1936 report stated, the Farm had "been a paying institution to the taxpayers of the state, not only to the fruit growers but to the consuming public. . . . The large quantity and assortment of fruits that it is now possible to produce in Minnesota makes it unnecessary to send out of the state annually many hundreds of thousands of dollars for similar fruits grown elsewhere."[13]

On Alderman's retirement in 1953, Dr. Leon C. Snyder, then Extension Horticulturist was chosen as the Horticulture Department head and superintendent of the Farm. Under Snyder's leadership, the Farm continued its fine work in fruit breeding and expanded research to include other plants. His vision was broad and his ability to generate interest in horticulture was great. During his tenure, fourteen fruits and three ornamental crabapples were released. He remained superintendent

Entrance to the Fruit Breeding Farm, now the Horticultural Research Center.

On July 18, 1930, superintendent Dr. W. H. Alderman (in knickers) spoke to a group of tasters at the Fruit Farm. He was touting the famous 'Latham' raspberry.

Professors Leon C. Snyder and T. H. Weir are examining a tree at the Farm. Weir was the superintendent. Snyder followed him and later became the first Arboretum director.

until 1970 at which time he turned his full attention to the directorship of the Arboretum.

Since 1982 Professor James Luby has been director of the Fruit Breeding Program. Always on the lookout for new and improved varieties, Luby and his staff have investigated fruits from around the world, both wild and cultivated, searching for plants that might thrive in the rigors of the northern climate. He has paid particular attention to the genetic composition of plants indigenous to cold climates. Researchers from the Horticultural Research Center collect seeds and plants from the wild to see if their genetic make-up will contribute to winter hardiness, disease resistance, and/or productivity. Minnesota strawberries, grapes, and blueberries have all been improved with the injection of "wildness" into their makeup.

Luby is particularly interested in the possibilities of the apple. "Genetic diversity in the cultivated apple," he explained, "has been continually eroding from a point when more than seven thousand commercial cultivars had been described (1804-1904) to the present, when most of the world's production is based on two cultivars, 'Delicious' and its red sports, and 'Golden Delicious' and its seedlings."[14]

In pursuit of diverse genetic material, Professor Luby, with a team from the United States Department of Agriculture, traveled to Kazakhstan in 1995 where, for one month, they explored the wild apple forests in the eastern mountains. Kazakhstan is important because its climate is similar to that of Minnesota, with cold winters and comparable rainfall. Before the break-up of the Soviet Union, the area was closed to Westerners, and for that reason, few of its apples made it to North America. There is enormous genetic diversity represented in these forests—scientists speculate that the apple tree originated here—but due to population and economic pressures, the area is gradually being turned over to other ventures. Therefore, it was important to make timely collections before much material was lost to development.

Kazakhstan's ancient forests are filled with three-hundred-year-old trees unlike any seen in the United States. Some have branches sprawling on the ground; others are themselves low shrubs. Some bear apples as small as cherries, others the size of baseballs. The fruit comes in yellow, white, purple, and orange as well as red tones; and oblong and conical shapes as well as round. "While some are decidedly sour and astringent," said Luby, "others were brilliantly sweet with hints of berry-like flavors. Perhaps most important, some may be resistant to the orchardist's worst nemeses: apple scab, apple maggot, and codling moth."[15] The expedition collected about sixty thousand seeds and germinated over two thousand of them which were then evaluated in test orchards at the Horticultural Research Center to determine which might be used in further breeding.

Similarly, to expand the genetic makeup of strawberries, Luby joined a team from the National Clonal Germplasm Repository, and in 1985 and 1989 this group collected seeds, clones, and herbarium specimens of wild strawberries in the western United States. Researchers at the University of Minnesota have systematically crossed the best of these with the best domesticated ones for a better fruit. In addition, wild blueberries collected by Dr. Cecil Stushnoff became foundation stock in the blueberry effort. Wild grapes, collected from Minnesota and Manitoba and evaluated by former staff members Elmer Swenson and Patrick Pierquet were the source of winter hardiness in recent wine grape introductions.

In the early years, the Fruit Breeding Farm made no concentrated effort to find new plants that were strictly ornamental. However, in the course of Fruit Breeding work, several did appear. Three were named and introduced: the 'Flame' crabapple (1934), the 'Manitou' almond (1923), and the 'Newport' plum (1923).

During his tenure as superintendent of the Farm, Dr. Snyder was very interested in evaluating plants for use in Minnesota landscapes. One of his first efforts was to plant shrubs and trees on the grounds around his cottage at the Fruit Breeding Farm. Soon his ornamental experiments outgrew the space there, and he developed a testing program on some of the Farm's larger fields.

The 1954 annual Minnesota State Horticultural Society's Fruit Breeding report noted that ninety arboreta, botanic gardens, and experimental stations were testing and hybridizing ornamentals. In Canada the experimental station at Morden, Manitoba, had more than two thousand species and varieties of woody plants in its testing program.

Very little of this work had been done in Minnesota, the report noted, "one of the most northern states where it is if anything most needed."[16] Frequently Minnesota nurserymen were obliged to travel to Morden to select hardy ornamentals for their nursery trade. The report noted how valuable such work would be for farms, homes, and parks.

In 1954 the Woody Landscape Breeding Program was initiated at the Farm, a natural outgrowth of Snyder's passion. By 1955 he and the staff had acquired from botanic gardens, nurseries, and experiment stations more than six hundred species and varieties of trees and shrubs to trial that were planted in test areas at the Fruit Breeding Farm and at several University of Minnesota experiment stations. Work was begun on an ambitious list of plants: rhododendrons, azaleas, privets, hollies, forsythias, daphnes, boxwoods, maples, dogwood, viburnums, flowering crabs, weigelas, and caraganas.

The 1957 annual report commented that hundreds of trees and shrubs were being grown under careful observation, many of which were not indigenous to the state. A year later the report noted concrete results,

and in 1958 the 'Radiant' crab, a flowering tree, was introduced. Two shrub roses, 'Prairie Fire' and 'Viking Queen,' soon followed. The founding of the Minnesota Landscape Arboretum in 1958 insured additional space for the observation and testing of plants.

The year 1954, when Dr. Leon Snyder became head of the Department of Horticulture, is generally recognized to be the official beginning of the Woody Landscape Plant Breeding Program. Snyder had the ability to see needs and recognize opportunities, and he had the

The Arboretum's iconic Red Barn was constructed in 1920 on the Williams Farm; this property is now part of the Minnesota Landscape Arboretum.

NORTHERN TREASURE

talent for exciting others—amateurs and professionals alike—to pursue the goal of a wider plant palette.

When Snyder envisioned the Arboretum's mission, he had several objectives in mind: to provide a laboratory for the development of new ornamentals through a breeding program, to serve as an outstanding laboratory for students of horticulture, and to introduce new plants to the area.

As head of the Horticulture Department, Snyder had hired Albert G. Johnson to breed woody landscape plants, and soon after the first land was purchased for the Arboretum, Johnson's breeding work was moved there. His most famous effort, the crossing of *Rhododendron X kosteranum* and *Rhododendron prinophyllum* in 1957, resulted in the Northern Lights Azalea F1 hybrid. This hardy plant was extremely floriferous with fragrant pink blossoms, and since its formal introduction in 1978, twelve more cultivars in pink, lilac, rose, yellow, orange, and white have been added to the series. In other efforts, Johnson, often in collaboration with extension faculty Mike Zins and Mervin Eisel, searched the region for new woody plant materials which are still being evaluated by researchers at the Horticultural Research Center.

Dr. Snyder also recognized the value of native plants. From a native seedling population growing just northwest of Duluth, he selected the original 'Northwood' maple. The red maple (*Acer rubrum*) is highly valued as a landscape tree through much of the eastern United States for its silver-gray bark and spectacular orange-red fall color. Although most cultivars are not hardy enough to

withstand the severity of Minnesota's climate, because of its northern origin, this maple, released as 'Northwood' in 1980, is well suited for this region's conditions.

In 1967 the Fruit Breeding Farm was renamed the Horticultural Research Center to reflect the expansion of its mission to include its increased research diversity. In 1987 the HRC merged administratively with the Minnesota Landscape Arboretum, reflecting the long cooperative nature of the two institutions and increasing the efficiency of their joined operation.

Dr. Harold Pellett became director of the Woody Landscape Plant Breeding Program (WLPBP) in 1978. His tenure was a very productive one in which facilities were updated, research broadened and many new plants released. Pellett and fellow HRC scientists focused their research on dogwood, viburnum, mock orange, forsythia, honeysuckle, rose, birch, and azalea. He is perhaps best known for one of his earliest projects at the University—the development of the acclaimed Lights series of azaleas from the initial Northern Lights cultivars.

In 1996, on a trip to Asia in search of plants which would thrive in Minnesota's climate, he and a USDA team ventured into the mountains of Kazakhstan and collected seeds of wild trees, shrubs, and a few herbaceous plants—all of which were acclimatized to cold and drought, making them potentially useful for Minnesota breeding.

Dr. Pellett did significant research on the effects of exposure on the winter injury of conifers and broad-leaved

Dr. Harold Pellett focused his work on woody landscape plants, among them viburnums, forsythias, and azaleas.

evergreens, as well as the effect on conifers of water stress due to drought. He also studied how factors such as shade, soil compaction, and soil temperature affect the growth of woody plants.

In 1988 Pellett and scientist Kathy Zuzek re-launched a rose-breeding/evaluation program aimed at developing shrub roses with an attractive plant habit, repeat bloom, hardiness, and disease tolerance. As part of their research, Zuzek and fellow scientist Steve McNamara studied the performance of shrub and old garden roses at the Arboretum and at a nearby private garden. Out of their research came the book *Roses for the North* in 1995.

During Harold Pellett's tenure, the Center named and released thirty woody landscape plants, many that are still industry standards including the 'Autumn Spire'

red maple, 'Northern Pearls' pearl bush, 'Emerald Triumph' viburnum, and 'Honey Rose' honeysuckle. His modest demeanor and strong work ethic contributed to his great success, and the techniques he developed and documented for testing the hardiness of woody plants are still in use today. For his breeding work Dr. Pellett has received more than ten major awards, including the American Society for Horticultural Science Distinguished Achievement Award for Nursery Crops, the Award of Merit from the International Plant Propagation Society, and the Garden Club of America's prestigious Medal of Honor.

Peter Olin, current director of the Minnesota Landscape Arboretum, sums up Pellet's contributions: "His introductions have been a tremendous asset to the nursery industry, adding a wide variety of useful and hardy landscape plants."[17]

The work of Albert Johnson and Harold Pellett has resulted in stunning azaleas that are winter-hardy for the northland.

BUILDING

CHAPTER THREE

LAUNCHING AN INSTITUTION as ambitious as the Minnesota Landscape Arboretum required the energy, imagination, and dedication of many individuals, plus a little bit of luck. Such a fortunate coalition of contributors and conditions came together in the mid-1950s, and the Arboretum was born.

"We must give credit to the Men's Garden Club of Minneapolis," said Dr. Leon C. Snyder, first director of the Minnesota Landscape Arboretum, "for having sparked the idea from the beginning."[1] The club's Tree and Shrub Committee felt that the Fruit Breeding Farm had done a great deal to improve Minnesota's agricultural offerings, and the men thought the state needed a comparable facility to study woody plants for their landscape use. They approached the Minnesota State Horticultural Society with a proposal, the Society agreed, and in January 1955 a state-wide committee was organized to study the feasibility of an arboretum and to search for an appropriate site. Archie Flack was appointed chairman of the "Landscape Arboretum Project," and in March of that year the committee presented its three conclusions to the Society: (1) the variety of woody landscape materials in Minnesota was limited, (2) modern architecture required the use of a wider selection of compact trees and shrubs, (3) a broader research program was necessary to guide the way toward the improvement of woody plants. Snyder reported that the University of Minnesota had given its permission to proceed, and with the Society's blessing, the group moved ahead promoting the arboretum idea, raising funds, and looking for a site.

The name selected for this endeavor was "Landscape Arboretum," an appropriate choice since the Arboretum's early leadership focused on the testing and evaluation of trees, shrubs, and other ornamental plants for landscape use. And unlike other arboreta such as the Arnold Arboretum of Boston, the Landscape Arboretum would contain herbaceous plants and shrubs, not simply trees or plants grown primarily for botanical study.

THE LAND

After much discussion and evaluation of possible locations, a site on Highway 5 near the Fruit Breeding Farm was selected. The spot provided easy access to the equipment, facilities, and staff of the Farm, and it would allow the work on ornamentals to move easily back and forth between the two facilities. The location was within reach of both Minneapolis and St. Paul; the owner, Dr. Herbert J. Berens, was interested in selling the property to the arboretum; and, of considerable importance, it was a naturally beautiful area with a varied terrain.

The site included nearly one hundred acres of wooded land, fifty acres of open, rolling land, and two lakes. While the native trees and wildflowers would lend interest as new plantings were developed, the lakes and marshlands could provide a natural habitat for aquatic and moisture-loving plants. The soil was fertile. The option to purchase was to be $1,000 and the purchase price $35,000. Accordingly, in June 1956, Mrs. Grace B. Dayton provided the option funding, and the Arboretum Committee and the Horticultural

Society continued with promotion and publicity.

Unfortunately, at the end of one year, the Society had raised only $7,137 toward the purchase price. "And so, it began to look a little bit bleak," Snyder said.[2] Dr. Berens allowed the option to extend another year, giving the group a reprieve.

Deciding that the Arboretum project was too important to fall by the wayside, several officers of the Lake Minnetonka Garden Club offered to help. The women, led by Mrs. John (Eleanor Lawler) Pillsbury, Mrs. Frederick C. (Clara Cross) Lyman, and Mrs. Cargill (Pauline Whitney) MacMillan, held a dinner and invited their husbands. At every place lay a pledge card, indicating the amount each couple was expected to pay. By the evening's end, the group had oversubscribed the purchase price and the acquisition was assured. On February 6,

1958, the land was turned over to the University, and the dedication followed later that year on September 6.

"Once it was known that we had the land," explained Dr. Snyder, "everybody wanted to help, and in just a few months more [money] came in without much effort."[3] A grant from the Hill Family Foundation added $60,000 for research. With the thousands of additional monies given by others, the Arboretum made improvements: a gravel road, picnic tables, a water system, and land clearing. Edwin Lundie, renowned local architect, donated his services, designing a picnic shelter in 1962, trellises and a pump house in 1964, and an entrance sign in 1965.

From its inception, the Arboretum had two main goals, research and education. Quoting Dr. Snyder: "The original purpose was to test woody plant materials from all parts of the world for adaptability and

In the early years, folks toured the Arboretum via tractor. Here in 1958 a group views the area along Three-Mile Drive.

landscape use in Minnesota and through a breeding program to develop new cultivars of plants."[4]

In accordance with these goals, planting began in earnest as soon as the land was acquired. Flowering crabapples (over fifty different cultivars), pines, apricots, maples, and the azaleas for the breeding program were some of the first. The planting plan was developed by the landscape architectural firm of Hare & Hare of Kansas City, Missouri, and by 1959 the plantings totaled nearly 2,000, representing 580 species and horticultural varieties.

PLANTING THE FIRST TREE

ACCORDING TO DR. SNYDER, the first planting was actually made before the property was acquired. The Fruit Farm had obtained seeds of Peter Gideon's shellbark hickory (*Carya lacinosa*) and planted them along Lake Tamarack. Clearing that land in the summer of 1957, workers had dug up one of the trees and left it to languish in a wheelbarrow. Snyder happened along, and "thinking to give it a decent burial," he recalled, took it to the Berens' property. "Well, now if I were a hickory tree," he asked himself, "where would I want to be planted?" He decided on a hilly spot near the present nut collection.[5]

"Now everyone knows," Dr. Snyder continued, "you can't transplant a hickory tree even at the best time of the year. Well, that tree didn't know it couldn't grow and is today one of the most beautiful trees in the Arboretum." This item of Arboretum history was known only to Snyder, he recalled in 1983.[6]

This shellbark hickory, planted by Dr. Snyder in 1957 before the Arboretum opened, still thrives on a hill near the Nut Collection.

Of the original property, only about eighty acres were cleared and appropriate for planting; the remainder were wooded with a native stand of maples. Within five years, all usable land had been filled and the need for additional land became apparent.

The first piece that became available was the ninety-seven-acre Williams Farm located south of the original Berens property. The Saint Paul Garden Club, led by Mrs. Charlotte Ordway, offered to provide the necessary funds, and the club quickly raised the asking price of $45,000 and much more. The additional dollars were used to help fund the azalea breeding project.

During 1963 the forty-five-acre Hermann Farm, just to the west of the Arboretum land, was acquired as a gift from Mrs. Katherine Decker Winton and Mr. and Mrs. Russell Bennett. On part of this property, the Arboretum reconstructed a tall-grass prairie resembling one which might have existed before Europeans arrived in Minnesota.

For the next ten years, the Arboretum grew steadily, expanding to 576 acres by 1972. "There was never a master plan for land acquisition," Dr. Snyder said in 1983. "We've taken the opportunity to acquire adjoining land as it became available and we felt we could handle the purchase. I don't think at any time we paid more than the market value and often got a very favorable price."[7]

Little land was added during the next two decades; however, as development began to encroach, the Arboretum found it prudent to acquire buffer zones. By 2006, its total acreage, including the Horticultural Research Center, was 1,047 acres. The facility was loosely bounded by Highway 5 on the north, Highway 41 on the east, 82nd Street on the south, and Bavaria Road on the west. The HRC operated on several sites, two of which were north of Highway 5.

STRUCTURES

Stylistic elements of the Arboretum can be attributed to the well-known local architect, Edwin Lundie. From the beginning Lundie took an interest in the Arboretum's development and lent his services free of charge. His stamp is there in the old entrance sign, the Ordway picnic shelter, and the Wilson Rose Garden trellises and pump house. The original Education (Snyder) Building is his, and the newest building, the Oswald Visitor Center, also echoes "Lundie design" characteristics.

Called the "grand old man" of Minnesota architecture, Edwin H. Lundie apprenticed with both Cass Gilbert, architect for the Minnesota State Capital, and with Emmanuel Masqueray, architect of the St. Paul Cathedral. By 1922, then thirty-one years old, Lundie had opened his own practice in St. Paul. Eschewing the pursuit of large corporate clients, Lundie preferred to design residences, cabins, and a few public buildings.

Rejecting the modernist style of many of his contemporaries, Lundie drew on historic and regional inspiration for his designs and used local materials in his work. These cozy, romantic places fit snugly into their environments, just as the Snyder Building nestles into the adjoining hillside. Lundie's work is characterized by attention to detail and expert craftsmanship.

Dedicated in 1974, the Leon C. Snyder Education and Research Building was designed by architect Edwin H. Lundie.

The Leon C. Snyder Education and Research Building is a quintessential Lundie construction, designed in his last years, beginning in 1966. Indeed, he died on January 8, 1972, before construction was completed. An adaptation of a European country manor, the building was six years in the planning. Construction started in 1971 and it was dedicated in 1974. The cost of $1,500,000 was donated by over five hundred individuals, corporations, and foundations in a campaign spearheaded by John E. P. Morgan, a civil engineer

who had built Sun Valley for the Harriman family and spent the rest of his life helping the Arboretum.

The buff-colored Pennsylvania brick, gray-stained wood, and gabled roof lines give the appearance of great age and stateliness. Interior details include massive Douglas fir timbers, brick fireplaces, white pine paneling, and hand-carved panels above the entry doors. On the south side, a blue stone terrace leads to the gardens. The terrace is a memorial to the enthusiastic fund-raiser

Set off by massive tulip plantings, the Snyder Education and Research Building, on the left, and the Oswald Visitors Center,

Morgan who died before the building was completed.

Within the building, a tea room, auditorium, gift shop, offices, and a library provided a hub for the Arboretum's activities and business. For three decades the beloved spaces ably hosted teas, classes, retreats, weddings, craft and book sales, and research. But as the Arboretum's membership, staff, and events expanded, the Snyder Building eventually proved too small to accommodate all people and activities. Membership had grown to over 18,000 and the number of yearly visitors to over 250,000. A larger auditorium and restaurant were needed as well as an expanded gift shop and more classroom and exhibit space. In 1998 the architectural firm of Ellerbe Becket was called upon to develop a master plan, including a new visitor center.

From the fall of 2003 to January 2005, the center was under construction. The new forty-five-thousand-square-foot building was designed by Rafferty Rafferty Tollefson Architects AIA; associate architects, SALA Architects; architectural consultant Scott Berry;

and landscape consultant Bryan Carlson.

Dedicated on May 1, 2005, the Oswald Visitor Center was named for Charles W. Oswald who, in honor of his family, made the major gifts toward the construction of the building and the development of the surrounding grounds. Oswald and numerous other donors generously contributed a total of twenty million dollars to make the facility possible.

"Key goals in designing the building," explained Arboretum director Peter Olin, "were to minimize the impact of its size and to create a compatible relationship with the Snyder Building."[8] Elements which echo the Lundie style are the Douglas fir timber trusses, broken roof lines and dormers, warm earthy colors, fireplaces, and buff-colored brick. New features are large windows and skylights which allow maximum light to enter and allow visitors to view the gardens. A sophisticated energy system, using geothermal energy for heating and cooling, helps to minimize the building's environmental impact, and an automated

above, illustrate the Old World charm introduced by Edwin Lundie and carried forward by Rafferty Rafferty Tollefson Architects.

lighting system, which responds to exterior light conditions, reduces energy costs.

Visitors enter through the McQuinn Great Hall. Featuring a soaring forty-foot ceiling, this large, dramatic space showcases structural Douglas fir timbers and porcelain floor tiles. Just beyond, the Reedy Gallery provides space for an ever-changing slate of art, generally nature-themed. The 375-seat MacMillan Auditorium, the Wall Education Wing with two high-tech classrooms and a teaching garden, a large dining room, and a spacious gift store make the Center a well-used space. Surrounding the building are welcoming terraces and colorful entry gardens designed by landscape architect John Larson of the SRF Consulting Group of Minneapolis.

As the children's gardening programs expanded, so too grew the realization that a building was needed to accommodate all their activities. Generous donations from Marion and John Andrus III and the Donald T. Knutson family enabled the project to move forward, and in 1982, the ground- breaking took place. The 4,300-square-foot building, designed by

Bruce Knutson, was dedicated in June 1983.

To accommodate an experiential learning approach, the building included a greenhouse and was close to the gardens; a large talking tree in the entrance hall welcomed the visiting children; and there was room for microscopes, pots and seeds, laboratories, staff offices and storage.

Within fifteen years, however, the children's programs had once again outgrown their space, and in early 2001, Oertel Architects, a St. Paul firm, was commissioned to plan an addition and a remodel. Named the Marion Andrus Learning Center and the Sally Pegues Oswald Growing Place for Kids, the 12,000-square-foot facility has redesigned classrooms, hands-on laboratory and kitchen facilities, additional greenhouse space, interactive teaching exhibits, and a teacher resource center. Funding was provided by the Andrus family, Charles W. Oswald, Robert and Sally Hebeisin, William and Helen Hartfiel, Conley and Marney Brooks, and the Neilson Foundation. The new building, with easy access to the gardens and a harvest kitchen, connected the whole process from growing seeds to food preparation.

The Marion Andrus Learning Center and the Sally Pegues Oswald Growing Place for Kids.

The Berens Cabin has played an important but changing role in the Arboretum through the years. Surrounded by 160 acres, the cabin (see p. 42) was originally the summer home of Dr. Herbert Berens whose family had built a one-room cabin in 1940, and added a kitchen and bedroom later. Once the land belonged to the Arboretum, the cabin housed summer employees and volunteers. Dr. Snyder had an office there, tour guides were headquartered there, and visitors stopped in for information about the Arboretum and its programs. Then for years it was used for storage.

In 2001 the Arboretum Auxiliary began a two-year restoration of the cabin involving the addition of a new frost wall footing, new roof and windows, painting, and light installation. Inside Auxiliary members created an interpretive exhibit depicting the history of the Arboretum in photographs and text, and the Men's Garden

Club of Minneapolis planted a shade garden on the grounds designed by landscape architect Eldon M. Hugelin and dedicated on October 17, 2003.

DIRECTORS

DR. LEON C. SNYDER, a native of Michigan, was born in 1908. He attended the University of Washington where he studied horticulture and botany. He obtained his bachelor's, master's, and doctoral degrees there, completing his studies in 1935.

After teaching at the University of Wyoming and South Dakota State College, Snyder came to Minnesota in 1945 as the extension horticulturist. In 1953 he became head of the Department of Horticultural Science and supervisor of the University Fruit Breeding Farm. He was named director of the Arboretum in 1958. By 1970 it became clear that the arboretum directorship required his full attention, and he was allowed to relinquish his duties as department head to devote all his time to the Arboretum. In 1976 he retired from the Arboretum but continued to write, teach, and volunteer there.

Dr. Snyder accomplished much in his lifetime. He taught students and home gardeners for fifty years, supervised horticultural research at the University, and wrote a weekly column for the Minneapolis newspaper. He authored four books—*Gardening in the Upper Midwest*, *Trees and Shrubs for Northern Gardens*, *Flowers for Northern Gardens,* and *Native Plants for Northern Gardens*—which have become classics. However, his most significant achievement was undoubtedly the launching and early development of the Arboretum.

Leon Snyder had the vision, the organizational skills, the meticulous attention to detail, and the passion to envision the project and bring it to completion. He was able to generate enthusiasm in others and make connections that enabled the Arboretum to succeed.

He was a hands-on director who spent several days every week maintaining the Arboretum grounds himself. Long-time staff member, Merv Eisel, wrote in

Dr. Leon C. Snyder, the first director of the Arboretum, on the steps of the Snyder Education Building.

VERA SNYDER

DR. SNYDER'S WIFE, Vera, was equally enthusiastic and contributed greatly to the Arboretum efforts. She shared their large and bounteous kitchen table with many and eased Saturday work days by providing coffee and cookies at 10:00 a.m. and at 2:30 in the afternoon. "She was indeed an asset to the whole project," Eisel summed up.[9]

Numerous regional and national awards bore witness to Leon Snyder's achievements. Among them were the Gold Medal Award of the Men's Garden Club of America, the Medal of Honor from the Garden Club of America, the Norman Jay Coleman Award from the nursery trade for his research, and the Liberty Hyde Bailey Award from the American Horticultural Society.

Dr. Francis de Vos was the Arboretum's second director. He extensively developed the site closest to the Snyder Building, adding the Wilson Rose Garden, the Japanese Garden, the Slade Perennial Garden, and the Home Demonstration Gardens.

1953, "Except for Saturday afternoons when the Gophers had home games, Snyder recognized no holidays or hours. I remember that he and I planted many of the azaleas in the Saint Paul Garden Club Azalea Collection on the fourth of July one year. Dr. Snyder's sole objective was to promote the Arboretum."[10]

DR. FRANCIS DE VOS had a long and distinguished career before arriving at the Minnesota Landscape Arboretum. He received his undergraduate degree in Horticulture from the University of Massachusetts, his master's and doctorate from Cornell. From 1951 to 1953, he served as horticulturist in charge of plant collections at the United States National Arboretum in Washington, D.C., and for the next fourteen years, he was Associate Director of Research and Education programs there. He

served as both secretary and director of the American Horticultural Society and as president of the American Association of Botanic Gardens and Arboreta. From 1967 until 1977, when he arrived in Minnesota, de Vos was director of the Chicago Botanic Garden.

Inspired by the fine display gardens of the Chicago institution, Dr. de Vos sought to bring more ornamental horticulture to the Arboretum. His first annual report spelled out his thoughts clearly:

The plants in our homes, our gardens, along our streets and our parks bring comfort, satisfaction and beauty to our lives. Arboretum displays that include: demonstration gardens with ornamentals, fruits and vegetables; varietal collections of annuals and perennials; turf plots; and house plants are representative of the broad scope of activities carried out by the Department of Horticultural Science and Landscape Architecture of which we are a part. I am confident that displays of this kind when developed in an overall setting of beautiful landscaped planting will meet the needs of students, faculty and the public to whom we look for support.[11]

Accordingly, de Vos authorized a master plan to be developed by the firm of Environmental Planning & Design of Pittsburgh, led by renowned landscape architect, John Simonds. Arboretum staff, the Department of Horticultural Science and Landscape Architecture at the University of Minnesota, and the Site Development Committee of the Minnesota Landscape Arboretum Foundation added their suggestions. From this grew the plans to intensely develop the twenty to thirty-acre site centered in the vicinity of the

McKnight Overlook. The Wilson Rose Garden, the Japanese Garden, the Home Demonstration Gardens, the Waterfall and Overlook, the Slade Perennial Garden, the Woodland Azalea Garden, and Herb Gardens were all included as part of this master plan. In addition, pedestrian walkways were redesigned to improve circulation and grades. The largest single development, which contains eight separate gardens with useful ideas for the home owner, was aptly named the Francis de Vos Home Demonstration Gardens.

On his retirement in 1984, de Vos could note with pride that many of the ideas and plans that were generated during his tenure had come to fruition.

PROFESSOR PETER OLIN was named Arboretum director in September 1985, following a nine-month appointment as acting director. Prior to accepting the directorship, Olin was a professor in the Department of Horticultural Science and Landscape Architecture at the University of Minnesota, a position he continues to fill. Olin's years at the Arboretum have been notable for growth in numerous areas: programming, garden expansion, building additions, and fund-raising.

A native of Connecticut, Olin earned his Bachelor of Science degree in Landscape Design and Ornamental Horticulture in 1961 from Cornell University. He spent a year at the University of California studying landscape architecture, and in 1971 received his MLA (Masters of Landscape Architecture) degree from the University of Massachusetts.

Some of the major accomplishments during his tenure at the Arboretum include the additions to the Andersen

The Arboretum's third director, Peter Olin. During his twenty-four year tenure, Olin has added many new gardens, created environmentally friendly parking lots, expanded educational offerings, and overseen enormous expansion and improvements of structures.

Library and the Marion Andrus Learning Center, the development of the Therapeutic Horticulture Program, model roadside plantings, and environmentally sensitive parking lots, including a rain garden lot and a run-off model. Also added were many new gardens including the Spring Peeper Meadow—an exemplary wetland restoration, Richard and Judith Spiegel Entry Garden, Bailey Shrub Walk, Clotilde Irvine Sensory Garden, Pillsbury Shade Tree Exhibit, and Sarah Stevens MacMillan Terrace Garden. Also under his tenure 137 acres have been added, bringing the total acreage of the institution to 1,047.

In addition, Olin has increased the Arboretum's international presence. Each year he leads several garden tours abroad, the proceeds of which serve two purposes. First, they enable the Arboretum to send scientists to distant parts of the world searching for plants that may have potential in the Horticultural Research Center's cold-hardy breeding programs. Second, the funds help the networking and research efforts of struggling northern gardens in Estonia and Russia. In Estonia, the Tallinn Botanic Garden and the University of Tartu's gardens have received help to rejuvenate grounds and facilities, and in Russia the gardens of the state universities of Petrozavodsk and Tver have benefited from Arboretum funds and expertise.

Of prime importance to the Arboretum's future was the design and construction of the Oswald Visitor Center. This forty-five-thousand-square-foot building added new classrooms, a larger restaurant and expanded gift shop, plus gallery and auditorium space. Under Olin's guidance the Minnesota Landscape Arboretum has become one of the major public gardens in the United States.

GENERAL DEVELOPMENTS

The thrust of development at the Arboretum has been one of growing complexity and increasing size in all its facets—land mass, membership, programming, staffing, and structure. At its inception the 160-acre facility had seven staff members, including one gardener, the superintendent, one plant breeder, and a receptionist. In 1959, the first full year the Arboretum was open to the public, about five thousand people came for a visit. A winding gravel road led through the fields and woods, plots of trees and shrubs were planted in family groupings, and there were ten picnic tables and a public lavatory. There were several hundred members (all the new ones being listed in the annual report), and

membership cost five dollars annually.

Gradually trails were constructed, parking lots built, plants were continually added to the collections, and guided tours were provided upon request. The facility was open from 8 a.m. until sundown seven days a week from early April to early November. The 1964 Annual Report noted that 25,000 people had visited the Arboretum that year and 632 new members had joined.

By the twelfth year, 1969, a full-time director was needed. The position was approved by the University of Minnesota Board of Regents, and Dr. Snyder was appointed. The staff had grown to twelve and included an educational programmer, Mervin Eisel, who, in his Report of Educational Activities, noted that 313 groups had visited that year, including the Garden Writers of America and the International Plant Propagators Society. In addition to the short courses and tours, a daylong program for professional maintenance men—the Shade Tree Maintenance Program—attracted 275 participants. Further, three shelters, several outdoor fireplaces, and numerous picnic tables on the grounds accommodated some four hundred visitors daily. Annual events included the Auxiliary's Fall Festival and Spring Plant Sale and the maple syrup sugarbush operation.

In 1981, the *Minnesota Landscape Arboretum News* was begun. No longer were members sent only the annual report once a year; they began to receive bimonthly updates with information about what had been accomplished as well as schedules of events and classes to come. With the new format, the schedule of classes was expanded. While previously three series of

In 2006 the theme of the Arboretum's summer exhibitions was "Secret Gardens." The stone bench was installed in memory of Ruth and David Paulson.

classes had been offered—spring, summer, and fall—in 1981, a winter series was added, increasing the classroom attendance 46 percent to 1,656.

Initially the Arboretum's main attractions were the Collections and the natural beauty of the site with its lakes, wildflowers and trees. A few gardens—including the annuals, shrub roses, and woodland gardens—were also installed. Several other gardens—a perennial flower border, herbs, and an iris garden—were added during the next decade.

Under the direction of Francis de Vos and later Peter Olin, the gardens grew in number and in importance to visitors. At the time of this writing in 2007, there are over forty of them with more in the planning stages. From the entrance at Highway 5 to spots along Three-Mile Drive, visitors can observe designed areas, parking lots are planted with colorful shrubs and flowers, and numerous urns and hanging baskets line the terraces and walks. The Trumpet Creeper Tram offers guided tours daily during the warm months. Although spring and summer remain the busiest seasons, programs are held year-round. In addition, numerous groups, horticultural and otherwise, rent spaces for weddings, retreats, and meetings.

The fall events, Spring Plant Sale, and maple syrup operation are still visitors' favorites, but they have been joined by others. Since 1984, the Auxiliary has sponsored an increasingly popular garden tour, one that spreads over four days. Orchid Lights, an evening gala first held in 1988, has become the Arboretum's single largest fund-raising event, featuring an elegant meal, music, and views of the gardens. Other well-attended offerings are the Ice Cream Social (a thank-you to members and volunteers), the Andersen Library Used Book Sale, and holiday teas. Membership has swollen to over 18,000 and annual visitors surpass 250,000. To support all this activity, the permanent staff is now more than one hundred strong, increasing to two hundred during the growing season.

GARDENS

CHAPTER FOUR

LOCATED AS IT IS in the Big Woods country and on the edge of the prairie, the Arboretum property is blessed with natural beauty. Early European settlers to Carver County noted the rich vegetation there. In 1856 Swiss-born immigrant Theodore Bost wrote of his land, now part of the Arboretum: "My woodland consists of sugar maples on the east, maple and basswood to the north, and beyond that, where most of the timber is, I have a number of fine oaks, some of them more than four feet in diameter, some walnut trees, some flowering shrubs, basswood, maple, red oak as well as white and black, red and white elm."[1] During a walk Bost came upon another idyllic scene:

I had been following an Indian trail when all of a sudden I came out on the shore of a pretty little lake about two miles wide and three or four miles long. The lovely virgin forest surrounded it on all sides; a short distance away a deer was grazing on the grass at the water's edge. But for me the most beautiful thing was that there was not a house in sight, not a sound to be heard other than the cry of some wild swans. The fish swam right up close to me looking for food.[2]

One hundred years later, Dr. Leon Snyder commented on the beauty he saw on Arboretum property: "The native trees and wild flowers add interest to the area while new plantings are developing. The hilltops command inspiring views of the countryside. . . . The two lakes and the surrounding marshlands provide natural habitats for aquatic and moisture-loving plants. The native oaks provide ideal shade and soil conditions."[3]

Arboretum landscapes in the twenty-first century still include the natural scenery that Bost and Snyder admired. But to this have been added reconstructed prairie, restored marshlands, numerous plant collections, and spectacular gardens. There are many vistas, be they wild or manicured, to please the most discerning eye.

ENTRY GARDENS

All who enter the Arboretum grounds, whether to savor the gardens, to attend a meeting, or to report for work, pass through the floriferous plantings on Alkire Drive, funded by Darrel Alkire. At Highway 5, a seasonal display brightens the entrance—thousands of pansies in the spring, annuals later. Flanking the drive are large swaths of colorful perennials—liatris, rudbeckia, and coneflower. The gatehouse itself is always adorned with signs of the season. There are perennials in summer, fruits of the harvest in autumn, and holiday greens in winter.

Around the Oswald Visitor Center, a variety of plantings welcomes visitors. Six terraces offer places to meet, relax, and rejuvenate. The spaces are unified by low stucco and stone retaining walls, trellises reflective of Edwin Lundie's style, and a variety of concrete terraces. Tall grasses separate the private spaces, the courtyards and benches from the busy public road and parking lots.

The Newton Dining Terrace provides attractive spaces for outdoor dining.

Several named areas are adjacent to the new Visitor Center. The Kathleen Wright Garden—named for a longtime Arboretum volunteer, employee, and foundation board member—is a peaceful, terraced area bounded on one side by a low, stone retaining wall and perennial plantings with mostly white blossoms. The terrace features three shades of gray paving in a geometric pattern, linden trees, and a pergola. Within this garden is the Kathleen Wright Meditation Garden with a stone terrace laid in a labyrinth pattern. A raised fountain bubbles gently.

The Sweatt Entry Terrace Garden—dedicated in August 2005 in memory of Margaret L. Sweatt by her family—includes an abundance of shrub roses, Margaret's favorite flower. Surrounding the terrace is a garden containing numerous perennials in blue tones, from the small blue fescue (*Festuca glauca* 'Elijah Blue') to the tall delphinium (*Delphinium* 'Pagan Purple').

The Newton Dining Terrace was donated by the Patricia A. Newton family. In this large, two-level terrace providing space for patio dining, lacy honeylocusts (*Gleditsia triacanthos inermis* 'Impcole') and little-leafed lindens provide a vertical focus and light shade. A granite fountain, stone walls, gray paving stones, and handsome planters make this a favorite spot for visitors.

The Dahlberg Welcoming Terrace is entered directly from the Oswald Visitor Center's lower level. This is the place where people gather to start their garden tour or to wait for guided tours. Given by Kenneth and Betty Jayne Dahlberg, it is a splendid introduction to the Arboretum grounds. Its exciting color scheme of maroon green, chartreuse green, and blue green allows the eye to dance over the landscape with excitement. Its

The Kathleen Wright Garden is a calm, enclosed space adjacent to the Oswald Visitor Center.

outstanding combinations of color, texture, and form lead visitors to the easy conclusion that the Arboretum is unique and will provide a pleasurable experience.

The Stephen F. Keating Terrace is the Visitor Center's front garden. A place to sit and unwind from a class, conference, or meeting, it will be in full shade when the ginkgo bosque matures.

Like most gardens, the Richard and Judith Spiegel Entrance Garden has evolved over time. The original entry garden of perennials was begun in preparation for the national Perennial Plant Association conference in 1995. Landscape gardener Duane Otto designed and planted newer, unusual perennials around the existing evergreens and trees at the entrance to the Snyder Building. The garden proved so popular that it remained after the conference. Dick Spiegel, one of Otto's faithful volunteers, and his wife Judith, an Andersen Library volunteer, decided to provide funds to expand the small border, making it a lavish welcome to visitors.

The Spiegel Entry Garden is a study in color, texture, and variegation. Handsome from a distance when the large block of color becomes more apparent and equally stunning when viewed at closer range, the garden provides an opportunity for visitors to observe interesting cultivars not commonly seen in perennial plantings.

SARAH STEVENS MACMILLAN TERRACE GARDEN

It is rare for gardens to successfully combine the donor's wishes, the designer's ideas, and the site's requirements. Yet the Sarah Stevens MacMillan Terrace Garden has done just that. Designed to be the Ar-

boretum's "Welcome" area, it stands as a showcase for the best of Minnesota flower gardens. Given in memory of Sarah Stevens MacMillan by her family, the terrace was designed by Minnesota landscape architect Jim Hagstrom.

"The garden was conceived as we stood and looked out at the landscape," explained Peter Olin, Arboretum director. "That makes it unique." Before plans were drawn, Olin recalled, "The MacMillans, Hagstrom, myself, and Arboretum Foundation Board members gathered on the terrace to discuss ideas."[4] The family knew that the site should be a garden, a destination. Hagstrom noted that the space should be opened up to reveal the Arboretum beyond, and during that initial conversation, he suggested moving the existing convex wall to create a concave wall set back from the edge of the present terrace. This new, low wall of softly aging brick became a handsome frame for the space. The Snyder Building and a row of tall tree lilacs frame the other sides. Enclosing the Terrace Garden has resulted in its becoming both a resting place as well as a gateway to the larger Arboretum.

Mrs. MacMillan's own garden—her favorite plants, her emphasis on pastels, and the English design—served as inspiration for the project. In the English manner, the garden is filled to overflowing, the flowers accented by a cool circle of emerald turf in the center, by the blue trap-rock pathway, and by the gray-pink wall. Weathered benches, inviting visitors to sit a spell, add a feeling of serenity.

The terrace looks stunning from spring with scilla, crocus, hyacinths, and tulips, through fall, when purple

The inviting Sarah Stevens MacMillan Terrace Garden, patterned after Mrs. MacMillan's own English-style garden in mostly pastel hues, exemplifies the best of Minnesota flower gardens.

asters and pink and white chrysanthemums come into their own. In early summer tall clusters of purple alliums stand like soldiers and deep purple salvia sway with the breeze. In high summer, delphiniums and coneflowers grow shoulder to shoulder with generous clumps of phlox, free-flowering annuals like 'Queen Cherry' cleome, and 'Nicki Rose' nicotiana. Graceful cosmos add color and fragrance. Hanging baskets and container plantings complement the borders.

"We didn't want just another perennial garden," Olin said. "We wanted this to be the best that Minnesota could offer, despite the vicissitudes of weather or hungry wildlife."[5] By its design, plant material, careful maintenance, and location, the Sarah Stevens MacMillan Terrace Garden has become just that. Mrs. MacMillan's welcoming spirit sets the tone for the space, its beauty greeting

visitors as they enter the Arboretum's many gardens.

WATERFALL GARDEN AND DWARF CONIFERS

Just past the Morgan Terrace and the MacMillan Terrace Garden, visitors hear the sounds of falling water. Around the curve, the water cascades over boulders, flows beneath the lower path and rushes into a series of holding ponds on its way to Green Heron Pond, a remnant glacial bog. Beside the stones, large and tiny conifers lend a calm presence to the scene. In summer this magical spot is a respite with its sprays of water and cool green plants, and in the winter the boulders are dramatic in the snow.

The original waterfall was built in 1976 with a donation from the Margaret Rivers Fund of Stillwater. Leon C. Snyder, Jr., a professor of landscape architecture at the University of Missouri and the son of Leon Snyder, the Arboretum's first director, was the designer and supervisor of the project. To create the proper scale, sizeable trees and evergreens were moved in, berms were built along the trails, and the dwarf conifers were planted. However, over time the area was undermined by water seepage, and finally, in 1999, it caved in.

The Margaret Rivers Fund again provided the needed monies, and with Minnesota landscape architect Jim Robin as project designer, the waterfall and surrounding area were made even more dramatic. From the headwaters on the hillside, the water makes a gradual descent, swirling between stones along the walkway and down a long slope in a series of waterfalls. Many visitors never venture off the Arboretum's main pedestrian path, but those who do can observe the stream in an increasingly secluded landscape from wooden overlooks or carefully placed benches. The water meanders across moss-encrusted boulders as trees sway overhead; visitors can savor the sounds and sights of one of the Arboretum's best features.

On the slopes beside the walkway are dozens of dwarf conifers. Because of Dr. Snyder's strong interest in these trees and because of their value in the home landscape, the Arboretum has maintained a collection of dwarf conifers since 1971. The collection was first planted on mounded earth with large field stones installed to create a proper setting.

Early annual reports repeatedly mention the public's delight with this collection. In 1971, the report reads, "Last spring we planted these raised beds with dwarf evergreens and suitable dwarf deciduous plants. The

effect has been lovely and we have had many favorable comments."[6] The 1973 report notes that we "continued to receive many favorable comments."[7] And in 1974 it is noted that "Interest in these plantings was very high; the need to expand this area to the east is being considered."[8] In response, with the addition of the waterfall in 1976, the dwarf conifer area, also designed by Leon C. Snyder, Jr., was expanded to the east.

As part of the waterfall reconstruction in 2000, the dwarf conifer collection was redesigned and expanded once again. The main collection is clustered among the rocks along the central pedestrian pathway, and then continues down the slope toward Green Heron Pond. Here, visitors can see a dazzling array of forms and colors including the pale green dwarf Japanese larch (*Larix kaempferi* 'Nana'), the golden Sawara false cypress (*Chamaecyparis pisifera* 'Golden Chain'), and the Canadian hemlock (*Tsuga canadensis* 'Moon Frost') looking like a small frothy Christmas tree. The various shapes include the low and sprawling—juniper (*Juniperus horizontalis* 'Blue Chip')—and the globular, such as the white spruce (*Picea glauca* 'Little Globe'). Backing the collection are numerous large conifers, e.g., the Sawara false cypress (*Chamaecyparis pisifera* 'Filifera Nana') and the Macedonian Pine hybrid (*Pinus peuce x parviflora*). At the corner of the dwarf conifers and the lily collection sits the stunning *Picea abies* 'Acrona.' With its beautiful deep pink cones in early summer, this Norway spruce probably elicits as much comment as any other plant in the Arboretum.

THE ELIZABETH CARR SLADE PERENNIAL GARDEN

In 1979, as he began his tenure as Arboretum director, Dr. Francis de Vos outlined his vision for the institution's

Waterfall Garden with the adjacent dwarf conifers is a magical respite in summer and a dramatic sight in the snow.

The beautiful *Picea abies* 'Acrona' with its deep pink cones elicits many comments through the seasons.

future. He urged that the Arboretum concentrate on "those plants which we chose to include in our every day environments" especially "displays that include: demonstration gardens with ornamentals."[9] The Elizabeth Carr Slade Perennial Garden was one clear response to that proposal.

The landscape architects for the project were Geoff Rausch and Missy Marshall of Environmental Planning and Design of Pittsburgh, Pennsylvania. Mike Heger, Arboretum landscape gardener, and Tom Brinda, landscape architecture student, laid out the original plantings. Over the years, landscape gardener Duane Otto has modified that plan. Funded by Mr. and Mrs. W. John Driscoll in memory of Mrs. Driscoll's mother, the Slade Perennial Garden was dedicated July 14, 1984, and this one-half-acre site has been a model and an educational tool for home gardeners ever since.

The garden was inspired by the tradition of European formal gardens and designed in quadrants around a circular pool and fountain. In its various landscaped settings, visitors can see shrubs, small trees, grasses, annuals, and perennials as well as aquatic plants. Placed in attractive relationship to one another, the plants and landscapes provide ideas to home gardeners.

The quadrants closest to the central pool are planted predominantly in blues and grays to make the pool appear larger. The far quadrants contain flowers of all hues. Within each section, plants are grouped for bloom and complementary color. Peonies, iris, and Baptisia might grow side by side, while 'Autumn Joy' sedums, asters, and a cluster of grasses might make

Inspired by European gardens, the Elizabeth Carr Slade Perennial Garden is designed in quadrants around a pool.

up another grouping. Middle quadrants of emerald turf set off the flowering plants.

In keeping with the garden's formal nature, there are small trees at each entrance. Two magnolias *(Magnolia x loebneri* 'Leonard Messel' and 'Merrill') stand at the western entrance; two apricots at the east *(Prunus* 'Sungold' and 'Moongold') and redbuds (*Cercis canadensis*) on the south. On either side of the stairs, lilacs (*Syringa meyeri*) are pruned onto a standard. Weeping crabapples (*Malus* 'Red Jade') flank the retaining wall, and a long row of the blue beech (*Carpinus caroliniana*) forms a backdrop hedge along the south.

Because the site is extensive, there are often numerous cultivars to observe. One could compare 'Northern

Fire' coral bells (*Heuchera*) with 'Brandon Pink,' 'Tattletale,' and 'Montrose Ruby' or see how *Nepeta siberica* 'Souvenir d'Andre Chaudron' and *Nepeta fassinii* 'Blue Wonder' differ. A visitor can also observe the differences between the following representative daylilies: 'Happy Returns,' 'Yellow Lollipop,' 'Bitsy,' 'Siloam Doodlebug,' or 'Green Glade.' Gardeners also have the opportunity to compare ground covers—observing colors and growth habits, understory plantings, or the shape of small trees.

The garden, which is handsome at ground level where details can be studied, is also stunning when viewed from the overlook on the north side. Its situation near the Snyder Building provides easy access, and it is not unusual to see visitors taking notes or questioning gardeners who are working the beds. Consistent plant labeling aids in making such learning possible.

HERB GARDENS

For thousands of years, herbs have been used for medicine, clothing, food, and religious ritual. Early American settlers brought herbs and herbals when they came to this country, to which they added the lore shared by Native Americans. In fact, whenever cultures meet, they exchange plants. The Arboretum's Herb Gardens, located adjacent to the Slade Perennial Garden, reflect the rich herbal heritage that is found in today's diverse society.

For decades, herbs have been on this site, an area added to Arboretum grounds in the late 1960s. In 1972 Herm Jeffers, a Twin Cities landscape architect, designed an herbal teaching garden with a knot garden feature near the dwarf conifers. This project was sponsored by the Twin City Herb Society and the Path Garden Club.

The array present today is the work of Geoffrey Rausch and Missy Marshall (formerly of Environmental Planning and Design of Pittsburgh, Pennsylvania; and today with the firm of Marshall, Tyler, Rausch, also of Pennsylvania). The core collection consists of the Kitchen Herb Garden, the Knot Garden, the Cloistered Garden, the Fragrant Garden, and the Dyers' Garden. The Gronseth Herb Garden is in the Home Demonstration Area.

Though each garden is separate, each is connected visually with similar hardscaping treatments. All areas are edged with brick, now moss-covered, and encircled with low retaining walls of limestone. Plants are clearly labeled for easy identification. The Herb Overlook, also called The Wedding Tower, was designed by nationally-known sculptor, Andrew Leicester. The two-story structure provides both a bird's eye view of the gardens and on the first floor, a cozy shelter or seating area with jars of herbs on the shelves. The Minnesota Herb Society funded the work which was completed in 1986.

In these gardens, the centuries roll back, and visitors see plants used by Elizabethans to sweeten the house or by medieval monks to cure insomnia. Generous support from the Minnesota Herb Society has insured that the gardens are always in peak condition. The Society contributes funds and volunteers for planting and hardscaping, and helps keep beds weeded and trimmed.

The Kitchen Herb Garden is a tidy collection of culinary herbs. To say there are oregano, basil, and thyme merely scratches the surface. In any one year, an entire bed may be devoted to varieties of parsley or oreganos, including golden, creeping, and 'Santa Cruz.' Of the basils, one might find lime, cinnamon, and 'Purple Ruffles,' among others. There are often wooly thymes, lemon thymes, and even oregano thymes.

To see the widespread use of herbs, the visitor need only notice the number of countries mentioned in their names. For example, there are French Sorrel, Vietnamese coriander, German chamomile, Egyptian top onion, and Greek, Cuban, and Puerto Rican oreganos. A short visit should inspire any cook to try yet another flavor.

The Knot Garden harks back to Elizabethan times when every estate included an elaborate garden of intertwined plants whose patterns are most visible when seen from above. In the Arboretum garden, visitors can climb the Wedding Tower or observe from the Kitchen Garden overlook.

The knot is set in the middle of a large brick circular terrace. The lines are made with Korean boxwood, dwarf red leaf barberry, lavender, germander, and hyssop. Many plants were tried before finding ones that would thrive in Minnesota's climate.

What will heal cuts and bruises or cure insomnia or strengthen the immune system? A slow walk through the peaceful Cloistered Garden will provide these answers and many more. Given by Loring Staples in memory of Mary Cushman Wells Staples and modeled after the gardens found in medieval monasteries, the area showcases plants used for medicine, food preservation, and flavoring. The arbor, covered with bittersweet and hops, lends a graceful ambience here.

As visitors walk through the Fragrant Herb Garden, the heavenly scents of damask roses and peonies waft by, and as one brushes against the borders, scented geraniums and artemisia release their fragrance. This garden includes the pungent—Russian sage and garlic, as well as the sweet—rugosa rose and mints. In 1996 Colston Burrell, an independent landscape designer, redesigned the space, creating a new walking path system which provides greater access to the plants.

The Dyers' Garden contains dozens of plants used in

The Kitchen Herb Garden includes culinary herbs from around the world.

The Knot Garden, harking back to Elizabethan times, is best seen from above.

making fiber such as flax, as well as plants used to tint, wash, or add fragrance to clothes. Shrubs, perennial vines, and annuals exemplify the large number of plants that have been utilized to make and color fabrics.

THE FRANCIS DE VOS HOME DEMONSTRATION GARDENS

Conceived as a dream of Francis de Vos, the second director of the Arboretum, the Francis de Vos Home Demonstration Gardens were planned to give home owners ideas that could be used in their own gardens. Most Arboretum collections were in grand, park-like settings, but these intimate niches clearly helped fill the needs of ordinary gardeners.

The original sites, dedicated in 1986, were designed by Environment Planning and Design of Pittsburgh, Pennsylvania, and contained nine separate spaces. The individual areas are unified by handsome gray wooden fencing and an overarching arbor structure. In speaking about the spaces, de Vos said,

Integral to the design are the landscape construction methods and materials that complement the plantings, frame the individual units, and provide the connecting links between the gardens. The designs and materials used in walkways, retaining walls, edgings, patio surfaces, and trellises are among the elements of garden architecture suggested to the visitor for use in his or her own garden. . . .

We are greatly indebted to our consulting landscape architect, Geoffrey Rausch of Environmental Planning and Design, for translating ideas into a landscape plan that will, as it matures, reveal a wonderful blending of sensitivity to the principles of design with the need for practical use.[10]

The Ludwick Naturalistic Garden, endowed by Dr. William F. and Harriet Ludwick, is a five-thousand-square-foot space replicating a naturalized backyard setting. Intended to be informal and low-maintenance, it is planted with woody and herbaceous plants. Native plants were chosen to provide year-round food, shelter, and nesting sites for birds. Some of the plants included here are meadow rue (*Thalictrum dioicum*), ginger (*Asarum canadense*), sweet fern (*Comptonia peregrina*), and hepatica (*Hepatica acutiloba*), backed by white pine (*Pinus strobus*). Borders are undulating, rather than geometric. A small patio and bench invite rest, and a sculpture, "Mother and Child," by well-known Minnesota artist Michael Price provides a focal point. The garden was redesigned in 2004 by landscape architect Kevin Norby.

The Fruit and Vegetable Garden offers an attractively designed, family-sized food garden. Featuring apples, pears, blueberries, strawberries, and grapes introduced by the University of Minnesota, in addition to a variety of common and unusual vegetables, the five-thousand-square-foot plot shows how much can be grown in a small space.

Fruit trees are espaliered against a wall to save space, and grape vines are spread across trellising. Here you can find six Minnesota apple introductions—'Sweet Sixteen,' 'State Fair,' 'Haralson,' Honeycrisp™, 'Keepsake,' and Zestar!™ as well as two cherry plums (*Prunus cerasifera* 'Compass' and 'Red Diamond'). In planting out the vegetables, landscape gardener Ted Pew uses different techniques each year such as companion planting, the French *potager* method, or square-foot gardening. The arrangement is stunning, and the main vegetable bed always includes the Garden for a Family of Four.

A cluster of cold frames, compost bins, the Keating Greenhouse, and a storage shed all demonstrate how desirable elements can be incorporated into an ordinary backyard. The greenhouse, funded by Stephen F. and Mary Keating, is often used to demonstrate potting

Director Francis de Vos planned the Home Demonstration Gardens to provide home owners with ideas for use in their own gardens. The Ludwick Naturalistic Garden is an informal area with undulating borders. The sculpture "Mother and Child" was prepared by well-known Minnesota artist Michael Price.

techniques for classes and to store some of the next year's annuals.

Just across the arbor from the food garden is the Edmundson Garden for Outdoor Living. Endowed by Dr. Hugh and Joyce Edmundson and intended to resemble a residential backyard, this comfortable spot includes the usual outdoor features of a home. There is a small lawn, ringed by trees and shrubs for privacy, and an exposed aggregate patio with outdoor chairs and a bench. Though it is not commonly used, the *Maackia amuren-*

sis was chosen as a pest-free tree with good shape which works well in the home landscape. Perennial and annual beds and container plants add beauty, and a low boxwood hedge helps define the space.

The charming Margaret and Harley Gronseth Herb Garden replicates the small formal gardens that have been planted next to kitchen doors for centuries. Only five hundred square feet and enclosed by a wooden fence and arborvitae hedge, the garden features a traditional knot design, geometric planting, and an alpine currant

The five-thousand-square-foot Fruit and Vegetable Garden showcases an attractive family-sized vegetable plot.

NORTHERN TREASURE

Colorful Rainbow Chard grows in the Home Demonstration's Fruit and Vegetable Garden.

(*Ribes alpinum*) hedge. Any pioneer would have been happy to have a well-stocked pantry of this garden's culinary herbs—basil, oregano, thyme, rosemary, sage, plus herbs for scenting the house like sweet Cecily and lemon balm. Brick paths and edging separate the beds and hedges, and a bench, backed by an espaliered apple, provides the visitor the opportunity to sit and enjoy the view.

Like a well-planned townhouse garden, the Garden for Small Spaces, funded by Lee W. Bachman in honor of Lee and his family, demonstrates that limited space can be both attractive and functional. In only nine hundred square feet, the space includes food and compact ornamental plants. In each of the four corners stands a small, flow-ering tree—an Oyama magnolia (*Magnolia sieboldii*), two gray dogwoods (*Cornus racemosa*), and a service-berry (*Amelanchier sp.*). Though small, the perennial beds feature plants with interesting foliage (*Heuchera americana* 'Pewter Veil' and *Pulmonaria* 'Spilled Milk') and bright bloom (coreopsis, Siberian iris, and Martagon lilies). Within a central square grow handsome salad vegetables like red lettuce, parsley and chard. A paved, brick area is enclosed by a hedge of alpine currant (*Ribes alpinum*) and boxwood, and behind the weath-ered bench, a blue clematis, 'Huldine,' climbs the wall.

In the small Cross Cutting Garden, named for and en-dowed by Marion Cross, there are spaces for perennials and annuals. The layout is a simple rectangle with easy access for clipping. Flowers are chosen for their long, sturdy stems and long-lasting blooms. The flowers vary from year to year but often include *Verbena bonariensis*, gladiolus and lisianthus. The perennials included are iris, baby's breath, asters, and lilies.

The Patio and Container Garden at the end of the arbor is a 1,500 square-foot area demonstrating ways to deal with balconies, decks, and patios which might occur in a home setting. A raised bed planted with annuals gives color all season long, while moveable containers and hanging baskets add bursts of color and texture. The

trees, ground covers and flowers here were all selected for their ability to tolerate the stress of container planting.

The two-thousand-square-foot Rock Garden is situated along the main walk and around a large deck. Three exposures help to create microclimates to showcase a variety of dwarf shrubs, conifers, and herbaceous plants. Weathered boulders have been placed to simulate natural outcroppings which provide an especially dramatic backdrop in May when spring bulbs and alpines burst into bloom. The Rock Garden Society of Minnesota helps maintain this garden of

The Margaret and Harley Gronseth Herb Garden, located within the Home Demonstration space and perfectly suited for a townhouse yard, is a small knot garden packed with culinary herbs.

NORTHERN TREASURE

small, sun-loving rock garden plants, as well as shade plants like ferns and epimediums.

Dr. Richard Behrens was a specialist in weed control at the University of Minnesota before he retired, and the Behrens Weed Exhibit, named for Behrens and his wife Anne, is an interpretive display of thirty-six weeds commonly found in Minnesota back yards. Here they are grown in raised cylinders, and the exhibit includes signs and information about eradication.

The Edna Downing Seasonal Display, funded by retired teacher, Edna Downing, features the All-America selections for each year and thus changes annually.

BURKE GRIGGS ANNUAL GARDEN

Displays of annuals have been part of the Arboretum's gardens since the earliest years. In Leon Snyder's 1973 annual report, he wrote, "This was an unusually good season for the annual flower display. The bloom lasted into November."[11] Earlier annual reports include photos of the formal beds which were grown near the Lundie trellises where the Wilson Rose Garden is currently situated.

The Garden for Small Spaces packs food and compact ornamental plants into a nine-hundred-square-foot area.

When the Wilson Rose Garden was installed, the annual beds were moved to a site just west of the Snyder Building at the beginning of Three-Mile Drive. To make way for the Oswald Visitor Center, the annual garden was moved once more. It is now permanently situated between the Slade Perennial Garden and the Oswald Visitor Center where its colorful blossoms are a bright welcome to the Arboretum's guests.

Todd Wickman, Minnesota landscape architect, was hired in 2004 to plan a formal garden with a stunning Merboy Fountain as its centerpiece. Several years previously, Dr. Virgil Fallon of Minneapolis had given the Arboretum this Victorian-style fountain which he had purchased at the Chelsea Garden Show in England.

Wickman's design incorporates circles and semicircles around the small pool and fountain. Sited on a gentle slope, the tiered garden is reminiscent of formal European gardens, its beds edged in granite and enclosed with circular stone walls. Duane Otto, landscape gardener, plans the annual displays with a yearly color scheme, one that is carried through the remainder of the Arboretum's annual displays. As in the other gardens, all the annuals are identified with tags for the education of visitors.

Minnesota landscape architect Todd Wickman designed the Burke Griggs Annual Garden with a Victorian-style fountain as its centerpiece. Each summer landscape gardener Duane Otto plans the displays with an annual color scheme, one that is carried throughout the Arboretum for the season.

The garden was endowed by the Mary Livingston Griggs and Mary Griggs Burke Foundation and opened in the summer of 2005.

SEISUI-TEI, THE GARDEN OF PURE WATER

"A Japanese garden is the expression of the essence of nature, not a reproduction of nature," said Koichi Kawana, a leading Japanese landscape architect and professor of landscape architecture at UCLA who designed the garden in 1985.[12] The generosity of John and Margaret Ordway made it a reality. In this Seisui-Tei, or Garden of Pure Water, Kawana crystallized the exquisite serenity nature can provide. Here, much is mystery and suggestion, leaving something for the viewer's imagination to provide. Ranked by the *Journal of Japanese Gardening* as one of the top twenty-five Japanese gardens outside of Japan, the garden has achieved much of the intention of its creator.

The approach itself, with thatched roof gate and softly mounded vegetation, hints that within waits a world apart. Structures, such as the garden house and entryways, are made from materials which harmonize and blend with the natural environment. Their shapes, colors and textures relate to the plants around them.

Kawana chose the stones, known to the Japanese as "bones of the earth," for their craggy shapes and intriguing textures, and using an ancient code to govern their placement, he arranged them precisely to evoke the feel of natural scenery. From the Arboretum's collections, Kawana hand-picked wind-swept pines which were then further pruned for a gnarled appearance. He chose plants in many shades of green to fill the garden,

using flowers and bright colors only for accents. From Japan, Kawana selected authentic, hand-carved stone accessories such as the lanterns, and he designed a naturalistic nine-foot waterfall to cascade into a koi pool.

All these elements have symbolic value in the Japanese garden. The pond symbolizes the ocean; the island represents a tortoise, meaning longevity and happiness. The larger stones near the waterfall's base represent a ship, signifying good fortune.

In a Japanese garden, the pine is the most important tree. Its cool, evergreen habit is the symbol of the eternal quality of nature. As its branches whisper in the wind, they express the unspoken wish for a long and happy life.

In the mid-1990s, after Dr. Kawana's death, Dr. David Slawson, a preeminent Japanese garden designer, became a consultant for Seisui-Tei. He has made a number of changes, adding blue/gray stone benches and removing overgrown vegetation. He widened the gravel path and replaced it with a gently curving aggregate one within which he placed small, flat stones, inspired by the "cat's paw" design around a seventeenth century tea house in Kyoto.

This subtle combination of greens and grays in rocks and vegetation has created a sanctuary, a cool retreat from a busy world. The garden is peaceful in all seasons—handsome in the green summer, sculptural in winter when the leaves have fallen. But it may be at its best in the mist. Then the plants blend together and the stones glisten like jewels.

Seisui-Tei or Garden of Pure Water was designed by Japanese landscape architect Koichi Kawana. The subtle combination of greens and grays in rocks and vegetation provides a sanctuary, a calm retreat from the world.

THE PAULINE WHITNEY MACMILLAN HOSTA GLADE

Creating a garden composed primarily of hostas is simple; creating one that is varied and interesting is more difficult. Here at the Arboretum, the Pauline Whitney MacMillan Hosta Glade succeeds with aplomb. Incorporating more than three hundred cultivars arranged in beds of different interpretive interest, the Glade is not merely an educational site; it presents a handsome landscape as well.

Originally begun in the 1960s with a clutch of donated plants, the garden is now one of the largest public hosta collections in the Midwest. In 1979 the collection was moved to its present location near the woodland entrance to the Japanese garden. The gentle slopes, mature maples, and curving paths make for attractive viewing, and the visitor can easily see why hostas, displayed here in all their lush variety, consistently rank as one of the top-selling perennials in America. Because of their versatility, they have become as popular with the novice gardener as they are with the expert.

Designated in 1980 as the first National Display Garden of the American Hosta Society, the beds are organized primarily by foliage color and form. There are eight different areas:

1. a bed made up of classic hostas—older, traditional cultivars
2. a bed of hosta species, from which today's thousands of cultivars have been developed
3. a landscape bed, incorporating hostas with companion perennials
4. an area of selected introductions from regional hybridizers
5. a display of fragrant hostas
6. a collection of plants named in The American Hosta Society's annual popularity polls
7. a planting of hostas for full sun
8. a border of blue hostas

The Hosta Glade offers a welcome respite from the summer's heat and a spectacular sight in autumn when the maples take on their fall color. A generous endowment in memory of Pauline Whitney MacMillan in 1990 assures that the garden will continue its tradition of excellence.

WOODLAND AZALEA GARDEN

"The Woodland Garden can be a nostalgic experience with its grove of sugar maples, wild flowers, woodland pond and naturalized waterfall," wrote Director Francis de Vos in 1986.[13]

The Woodland Garden was conceived as a part of de Vos's plan to bring beautiful spaces into the vicinity of the Snyder Building. Geoffrey Rausch, of Environmental Planning and Design, was responsible for the area's design. The site was dedicated in May 1987 and was sponsored by the Saint Paul Garden Club.

One of the largest public hosta collections in the Midwest with more than three hundred cultivars, the Pauline Whitney MacMillan Hosta Glade is a cool respite on a hot summer day.

This peaceful spot is modeled after a northern woodland garden and is planted with native trees, numerous shade-tolerant plants, and many of the Arboretum's Northern Lights azaleas, introduced in 1978. Several under-used plants such as the giant-leafed butterbur (*Petasites sp.*) and hardy winterberries (*Ilex verticillata* and its cultivar 'Afterglow') are also featured. The soft sounds of cascading water, the gentle motions of koi in the pond, and the canopy of trees overhead combine to create the tranquil setting.

The Howard Fern Walk, named in honor of the Charles Howard family and designed by Herb Baldwin, Twin Cities landscape architect, leads from the Woodland Azalea Garden, past a sculpture by local artist Katherine Nash to the secluded Woodland Pond. Along the pathway, visitors can see examples of numerous ferns and wildflowers.

GARDEN WALKS

A series of memorial walks above the Waterfall Garden provide pleasant strolling opportunities from spring through fall. In May, the Staples Lilac Walk bursts into fragrant bloom. This grassy walk curves between rows of numerous cultivars, unusual and oft-used. Given by Loring Staples in memory of Mary Peavey Wells Staples, the walk was dedicated in 1987. A bronze statue of Saint Francis by local sculptor Douglas O. Freeman was given in memory of Frederick B. Staples, Jr. by his family.

Soon after lilac season, the peonies begin their show along the Lang Peony Walk. Originally established in

Shown here ablaze in spring, the Woodland Azalea Garden is modeled after a northern woodland garden and planted with many of the Arboretum's Northern Lights azaleas.

NORTHERN TREASURE

1983, the collection of over two hundred plants includes many that are valuable in the home garden and others that have been lost to the trade. The plants are arranged on either side of a curving walk situated above the lilacs. Dedicated May 30, 1990 and named in honor of Helen Lang, the walk and peony collection were funded through the efforts of Theodora Lang with the Helen Lang Charitable Trust.

In summer the Lindquist Walk comes alive with the vibrant colors of lilies and later, dahlias. Russell and Avis Lindquist provided the funding for this area in honor of Russ's parents, Merieda and Arthur Lindquist, and Russ himself built the comfortable glider swing at the end of the walk, a great place to relax and view the gardens.

The Burdick Craddick Lott Walkway displays the best varieties of chrysanthemums and daylilies. Landscape architect Geoffrey Rausch designed the walks as part of the master plan developed under the direction of Arboretum director Francis de Vos.

It has been the goal of Director Peter Olin for the Arboretum to have an accessible walk (with a slope of 5 percent or under) somewhat parallel to Three-Mile Drive around the entire Arboretum, and segments are completed as funds are available.

The walks begin at the Dayton Wildflower Garden. The Hultgren-Haralson Walk extends the Wildflower Garden Walk to the Pillsbury Tree Walkway. This segment was donated by Jevne Pennock in honor of her parents, the Hultgrens, and her uncles, Charles and Fred Haralson, who ran the Fruit Breeding Farm in its early years.

Beyond the Pillsbury Tree Exhibit, the Blong Walkway connects to the Prairie Parking Lot. This segment was given in memory of Theodore and Doris Blong by their daughter, Ruth Haggerty, and her husband Dan.

From the Prairie Parking Lot the Frerichs Garden for Wildlife Walk connects to the Winton Walkway, named in honor of Mrs. David Winton on her ninety-fifth birthday and dedicated in 1992. This path in turn winds up to the maple collection and the Bailey Shrub Walk from the end of the Crabapple Collection.

From the Bailey Shrub Walk there is a section of unnamed walk to the Shrub Rose Garden and the Anne Barber Dunlap Walkway, a segment given in memory of Anne Dunlap by her many friends, which leads to the parking lot by the Dahlia Trials. New unnamed walks move from this lot to the Maze Garden, to the ornamental grasses, and to the parking lot near the hedge collection. Eventually this walk will come back to the Snyder Building.

THE PALMA J. WILSON ROSE GARDEN

When a beautiful site is matched with marvelous flowers, the result is lovely indeed. The Palma J. Wilson Rose Garden is just such a garden. Although not one of the largest rose gardens in the Midwest, this half-acre site at the Minnesota Landscape Arboretum is surely one of the most interesting, situated as it is on the side of a hill.

The roses here are excellent. Big and healthy, they are lovingly tended by the Minnesota Rose Society and the Arboretum staff. All are highly rated; most are All-America

In autumn, dozens of chrysanthemums bloom along the Burdick Craddick Lott Chrysanthemum and Daylily Walk.

Rose Selection winners. The view is amazing—a sweeping vista of the trees and fields beyond—but it is the elegant design, bringing flowers and hillside and visitors together in a most dramatic way, which makes the garden splendid. Three gentle tiers move down the slope. On each level, brick-edged beds and gray rock paths frame the roses, over six hundred of them. Hybrid teas, floribundas, shrubs, grandifloras, and tree roses—all in rectangular beds—are labeled for the visitor to enjoy.

In addition to rectangular pools and small fountains, a gazebo and benches contribute to the garden's serenity. Clematis, bittersweet, wisteria, climbing roses and other vining plants clamber up the handsome wooden trellises designed by Edwin Lundie. Here too grows the Anne M. Koempel Clematis Collection. With the Marilyn Nafstad Addition in 1992, dwarf and shrub roses were added and the garden became totally accessible to the

handicapped. This addition was designed by Damon Farber and Associates, local landscape architects.

The Wilson Rose Garden was dedicated in 1982, funded by Dr. John Wilson of St. Paul. As early as 1973, there were roses at the Arboretum because of the enthusiasm of Leon Snyder, a long-time member of the Minnesota Rose Society and its president in 1971 and 1972. Snyder envisioned the garden as a place to promote interest in roses and to educate gardeners on their care.

From the first, the Minnesota Rose Society has had a strong association with the Arboretum's rose garden. In addition to contributing much-needed funds, its members have tended the garden throughout its history, checking for disease and removing spent blossoms. In the fall they help prepare the roses for winter with the "Minnesota tip" technique, developed by Dr. Snyder, and in spring they come back to help uncover all the plants. Their devoted care, as well as that of landscape gardener Ted Pew, has insured that the rose garden is always a spectacular sight.

THE GRACE B. DAYTON WILDFLOWER GARDEN

The Grace B. Dayton Wildflower Garden is one of the oldest and most extensive gardens at the Arboretum. Given by her sons in honor of her birthday, this six-acre site of gentle slopes, woodland walks, and a meandering stream in a basswood, oak, and maple forest was dedicated in 1960. Openings support prairie and meadow plants; the streambed and pond edges, wetland vegetation. The native woods are home to spring ephemerals. Central to the garden in an area of acidic

The Palma J. Wilson Rose Garden with the Marilyn Nafstad Addition features over six hundred highly rated roses in brick-edged beds along a sloping hillside. The Minnesota Rose Society has helped maintain the garden since its inception.

soils grow wildflowers from northern Minnesota and Wisconsin. By 1997 the area had become severely degraded due to the loss of mature trees, which in turn caused stream erosion, flooding, and reduced wildflower populations. Mrs. Dayton's sons again stepped forward and provided the funds to renew the area.

Landscape architect Herb Baldwin and horticulturist Dennis Easley designed a totally accessible route through the garden, added two central gathering points, created a series of dams and small ponds, and installed an overflow drain to control water flow. New wildflowers and many native trees were planted where others had been lost.

Now this garden of varied plant life and quiet, undulating terrain attracts visitors for many reasons. Photographers set up tripods to capture seasonal blossoms. Bird watchers sit calmly to catch sight of the golden-crowned kinglet or the many hummingbirds. Those wishing to meditate gather quietly on the central brick terrace to collect their thoughts. Elders bring grandchildren to pass along their enthusiasm and knowledge. Gardeners come to find plants that will work well at home.

Here one can see many of Minnesota's spring ephemerals, those plants which bloom and set seed quickly before trees block the sunlight. Some of the first in March and April are blood-root (*Sanguinaria canadensis*) which forms a white carpet over a large area, yellow marsh marigolds (*Caltha palustris*) along the stream and woodland ponds, and the Minnesota dwarf trout lily (*Erythronium propullans*), a plant on the federal endangered list. The showy, white trillium

(*Trillium grandiflorum*) and the Virginia bluebell (*Mertensia virginica*) soon follow. In June, Minnesota's state flower, the showy lady's slipper (*Cypripedium reginae*) is in bloom alongside brightly colored, purple-fringed orchids (*Platanthera psycodes*) and cardinal flowers (*Lobelia cardinalis*). In August and September, visitors can see the closed gentian (*Gentiana andrewsii*) with its deep-blue petals.

The Arboretum staff, under the direction of landscape gardener Richard Gjertson, has worked to highlight less common plants. Through a series of "rescues," the staff has brought in the very rare snow trillium (*Trillium nivale*). This Trillium is a tiny plant, only two to three inches high, which blooms very early, often in patches of earth still surrounded by snow. The tall glade mallow (*Napaea dioica*) is another uncommon plant that has proved durable here, its panicles of white flowers bursting forth in July.

Structures in the garden blend unobtrusively with the natural world. Retaining walls are constructed of small boulders, steps from old tree stumps. Bridges are built of branches and logs, and benches are weathered. Although the main path is made of asphalt, auxiliary ones are of wood chips. Even Herb Baldwin's metal wildflower entry welcome signs are designed to rust naturally. These soft shapes and muted colors harmonize with the greens, grays and tans around them.

THE CLOTILDE IRVINE SENSORY GARDEN

On July 1, 1996, the Clotilde Irvine Sensory Garden and the Therapeutic Horticulture Program Center were dedicated, providing a setting for the Arboretum's new

In the Grace B. Dayton Wildflower Garden, spring ephemerals, including these yellow marsh marigolds (*Caltha palustris*), bloom before the trees leaf out and block the sunlight.

Therapeutic Horticulture Program. Visitors in wheel chairs can enter the Sensory Garden and see, on a smaller scale, many of the features found elsewhere in the Arboretum. The fully accessible garden was designed "to reflect the entire Arboretum in this space," explained Arboretum director Peter Olin.[14] The trees used are crabapples (*Malus* 'Prairie Fire'), reflecting the Arboretum's largest collection. There are annual and perennial gardens, a small rock garden, herbs, and water features. A bird and butterfly garden, dedicated to Adele Roller, attracts numerous winged creatures, and in a spot designated for art in the garden, various artists exhibit work created specifically for this site. The open-air structure and fencing are characteristic of the Arboretum's architecture.

The garden is designed to appeal to all the senses. The colorful tile didactics beg to be touched. When activated, they explain human sensory response. The three water features and the wind in the tall grass provide appealing sounds. The Sensory Wall Garden, funded by and dedicated to the American Academy of Neurology, is filled with fragrant plants and invites visitors to see, touch, hear, and sniff the leaves. A small rock garden in memory of Elizabeth and Charles Hodgman allows those in wheelchairs some challenge as they navigate a broken-stone pathway to the euonymus allée. This allée's only purpose is to lead the viewer's eye up into the deciduous Big Woods forest. The rock garden and allée were funded by Rusty Huff and dedicated in August 2000.

In addition, the Sensory Garden demonstrates the ways in which gardens can be made accessible. Hanging baskets can be raised and lowered. The ground-level bed is edged in brick, making it easy to find with a cane, and raised beds are constructed of various materials (concrete block, wood, exposed aggregate) to demonstrate ways the home gardener can accommodate special needs. The area includes a spacious open building that is home to many classes from both the Learning Center and the Therapeutic Horticulture Program.

In the spring many woodland plants like this ladyslipper (*Cypripedium reginae*) can be seen along the paths of the Grace B. Dayton Wildflower Garden.

Marjorie Pitz, well-known Minnesota landscape architect, designed the garden; architect and University of Minnesota professor Steven Weeks, the building. Olivia Irvine Dodge was the major donor, and the garden was named in honor of her mother. Funds from many friends, including the Arboretum Auxiliary, made this exciting garden possible.

ELEANOR LAWLER PILLSBURY SHADE TREE EXHIBIT

Any home owner looking to plant trees would do well to stop first at the Eleanor Lawler Pillsbury Shade Tree Exhibit. Designed to inform people about the important aspects of trees in our environment, the exhibit was installed in 1996, a gift of Eleanor Lawler (Mrs. John, Sr.) Pillsbury on her 100th birthday. The area was also designed by landscape architect Marjorie Pitz.

As visitors walk through the exhibit, they can observe numerous informational stations dealing with such topics as shade quality and tree shape. In the center an enormous tree house is a magnet for children and parents alike.

The youngsters can climb into a shaded playhouse or one baked by the sun, the thermometer mounted over the front door of each showing the temperature difference a tree makes. Parents can sit under an Imperial honeylocust (*Gleditsia triacanthos* var. 'Impcole') for light shade, a Kentucky coffeetree (*Gymnocladus dioica*) for dappled shade, or a *Tilia americana* 'Frontyard' linden for dense shade. What shape of tree might fit into the home landscape? Examples of several shapes—narrow, 'Princeton Sentry' gingko (*Ginkgo biloba* 'Princeton Sentry'); oval, swamp white oak

The Clotilde Irvine Sensory Garden provides a handsome spot that is fully accessible to visitors and participants in the Therapeutic Horticulture Program. This small rock garden allows those in wheelchairs to travel a path to the euonymus allée.

(*Quercus bicolor*); or pyramid, 'Greenspire' linden (*Tilia cordata* 'Greenspire')—illustrate various options.

Other educational displays deal with growth rate, sensory appeal, planting methods, and tree injuries.

CAPEN PRAIRIE GARDEN

Designed by landscape architect Jim Hagstrom, award-winning specialist in native plant landscapes, the Capen Garden serves as an entryway to the Bennett/Johnson

In the Eleanor Lawler Pillsbury Shade Tree Exhibit, installed in 1996, visitors enjoy the beauty of numerous trees such as this redbud (*Cercis canadensis 'Northern Strain'*) while learning important aspects of the various trees.

Prairie. This circular space, showcasing prairie natives for identification and educational purposes and demonstrating how beautiful a grouping of natives can be, contains a prairie spring bubbling down over limestone outcroppings to a small pool reminiscent of a Moorish garden. Further, an abstracted rivulet from a heavy prairie storm starts at the top of the center circle and winds down to disappear into the ground. At one side a pergola with seats serves as a place of rest or instruction. Constructed and endowed by Joan and Gary Capen, the garden was dedicated in the fall of 2005 in honor of Joan.

BENNETT/JOHNSON PRAIRIE

Stand in the Bennett/Johnson Prairie and the twenty-first

century falls away. Just a mile south, cars and trucks whiz by, and strip malls beckon. But here, the only sounds are the bees pushing in and out of the blue blossoms of bottle gentian (*Gentiana andrewsii*) or the gentle swish of big bluestem grass (*Andropogon gerardii*) as the wind passes through. Look up for the sight of the eight-foot-tall prairie dock (*Silphium terebinthinaceum*) with its nodding, yellow flowers and the equally tall compass plant (*Silphium laciniatum*) where chickadees and goldfinches feed. Among the blossoms of the butterfly-weed (*Asclepias tuberosa*) perch colorful butterflies, some of the forty-two species that feed on this plant.

Once, the North American prairies were our continent's

The handsome Capen Garden of native plants serves as an entryway to the Bennett/Johnson Prairie.

largest, most diverse ecosystem. Stretching from central Canada to the Mexican border, the prairies occupied more than a million square miles of what is now the United States. Today in many states less than one percent of the original prairie remains. In Minnesota it's less than one tenth of one percent.

When the Arboretum started its prairie reconstruction project in 1965, there were no other reconstructions in Minnesota and few in the United States overall. An expanding population was causing these native landscapes to disappear rapidly. Benefactors Mr. and Mrs. Russell Bennett and Mrs. Katherine Decker Winton purchased and donated the forty-five acres with five

used for reconstruction. In Albert Johnson, a taxonomist and research director at the Arboretum, the project had a passionate and talented leader capable of undertaking the rebuilding of a prairie.

Using seed collected from prairie remnants and hay cut from prairie relics in central and southern Minnesota, Johnson and volunteers scattered their findings thinly across the acreage. They also stripped soil from a prairie about to succumb to highway construction and spread it over the area, and in doing so, added insects and microorganisms as well as vegetation.

Prairie plants have extremely long roots and so can

survive a fast fire and drought. Thus, in the spring, to reduce the competition of weed species, Johnson began a program of controlled burns. A controlled burn simulates the fires that once whipped through this area, and in addition to killing weeds, the fire also warms the soil, stimulates germination, and frees nutrients from dried plant material.

Johnson's pioneering efforts set a high standard which landscape gardener Richard Gjertson maintains to the present. Besides continuing to reseed more native plants each year, individuals hand-weed exotics, especially sweet clover. Arboretum workers rotate mowing and burning sections of what has become a site which now exceeds more than twenty acres. In addition, they work to rid the fields of noxious weeds like crown vetch (*Coronilla varia*) and reed canary grass (*Phalaris arundinacea*) and to remove unwanted trees and shrubs that have taken hold.

Today the Bennett/Johnson Prairie includes marshy and dry areas, slopes and level terrain. Visitors can view a wet prairie with golden Alexander (*Zizia aurea*), meadow rue (*Thalictrum dasycarpum),* and tufted loosestrife (*Lysimachia thyrsiflora*) and see cordgrass (*Spartina pectinata*) with its fountain-like leaves. The mesic or middle area is bright with early goldenrod (*Solidago nemoralis*) and blazing star (*Liatris*). In summer, big and little bluestem grasses (*Andropogon gerardii* and *Schizachyrium scoparium*) toss with the breeze, and during autumn in the dry upland section, sideoats grama grass (*Bouteloua curtipendula*) can be seen with its delicate seed heads hanging all on one side of long, arching stems.

Mown paths weave through the low and upland areas, giving strollers a view of the fields of waving grasses and splashes of wildflowers. At the prairie overlook, visitors can take in the whole sweep of the land from the savanna with its gnarled bur oaks to the small pond surrounded with blue flag, and the wide, open prairie allows clear vistas for bird watchers.

THE JOHANNA FRERICHS GARDEN FOR WILDLIFE

The four-acre Johanna Frerichs Garden for Wildlife is designed to demonstrate habitats that attract animals, birds, butterflies, moths and bees by providing the water, shelter and plants they prefer. Animals such as woodchucks and rabbits, which might be considered a nuisance in other parts of the Arboretum, are tolerated happily here.

Visitors enter by a handsome wooden bridge across a small stream, and from there, a quarter-mile paved loop curves through the garden, taking viewers past model landscapes featuring various wildlife habitats. These model landscapes—including shrubs, a rock wall, a planting of native wildflowers for sun and another for shade, and a mixture of trees, shrubs and perennials— offer ideas for homeowners who want to attract wildlife to their own yards. In addition the loop is planted with fruit and nut trees for food and conifers for cover.

The paved path is a connecting link in the Arboretum's pedestrian pathway system. At the western edge, the garden connects to the Bennett/Johnson Prairie; on the eastern side, to the crabapple collection.

The garden's benefactor is Johanna Frerichs, whose

A hike through the stunning Bennett/Johnson Prairie with its tall grasses and bright blossoms allows visitors to experience the Minnesota prairie as it might have looked before European settlement.

gifts funded the start-up and will help maintain the garden in the future. Designed by Minnesota landscape architect Jim Robin, the garden was dedicated in August 2002.

HIGHPOINT ENDOWMENT CIRCLE AND ANNE DOERR MEMORIAL GROVE

At the Arboretum's highest point, overlooking the collections, research plots, and hillsides, sits the Highpoint Endowment Circle within the Anne Doerr Memorial Grove. Dedicated in June of 1995, this area has created a contemplative spot to complement the view and to

recognize those who have given endowments for maintaining the gardens and collections. Here the inscription, "These special gifts cultivate the bonds between plants and people for generations to come," introduces a series of plaques honoring some of the Arboretum's generous donors.

GORDON S. BAILEY SHRUB WALK

Anyone who thinks Minnesota shrubs are limited to potentilla and lilac would do well to stroll through the Gordon S. Bailey Shrub Walk. Dedicated in August 2000, the Walk was designed by Jim Robin, long-time

Using model landscapes, the Johanna Frerichs Garden for Wildlife provides examples of habitats that attract animals, birds, butterflies, moths, and bees.

Gently winding paths lead through the extensive Gordon S. Bailey Shrub Walk, an area presenting many of the best shrub cultivars available for the home landscape, shown here with spring magnolias in bloom. (Magnolia '*Leonard Messel*' is in pink; Magnolia stellata 'Royal Star' is in white.)

practitioner and instructor at the University of Minnesota's Department of Landscape Architecture. Paying tribute to Gordon S. Bailey Sr., one of the stalwarts of Minnesota's nursery business, the Walk was funded by the Bailey family and the Minnesota Nursery and Landscape Association.

Gently winding paths lead through hundreds of shrubs from azaleas to viburnums. Visitors can see the unusual, like native silver buffaloberry (*Shepherdia argentea*) or the wonderfully variegated cutleaf elder (*Sambucus canadensis* 'Laciniata'), along with more familiar plants. There are settings for lovers of shade and sun, introduced and native species. The sloping site heightens the drama and visibility of the shrubs on display.

The Shrub Walk presents many of the best shrub cultivars available for the home landscape in this region. The winnowing process was long. Arboretum staff sifted through lists of plants, considering disease resistance, form, and landscape effect in making their

choices. Newer varieties were included, but most of the selections are those which have proven their hardiness over time.

Planners understood the difficulty of a homeowner trying to choose between shrubs lined up in a nursery, so here gardeners can observe how the plants will look at home in a landscaped setting, noting their ultimate size and form. Large didactics stationed throughout the display help visitors think about factors to consider in selecting shrubs for their own yards and designing their landscapes.

The Bailey Shrub Walk is a link between the Frerichs Garden for Wildlife and the Shrub Rose Garden in the accessible paved walk encircling the Arboretum.

SHRUB ROSE GARDEN

The layout is graceful, combining handsome details, abundant roses, and a stunning backdrop of mature trees, making the Shrub Rose Garden a beautiful display of the Arboretum's collection of old-fashioned and shrub roses.

Old-fashioned shrub roses have been showcased since the Arboretum's earliest days because of Dr. Snyder's long-standing interest in the plants and his desire to highlight roses that were hardy enough to withstand Minnesota's weather. In 1961 the present site was chosen and a collection donated by Mr. A. R. Blackbourn was added. The Kenwood Garden Club sponsored the project.

The area has been reorganized several times. In 1966, the Old Fashioned and Shrub Rose Collection, as it was then called, benefited from several improvements. A retaining wall was built in a semi-circle behind the beds, and wooden trellises designed by Edwin Lundie were installed to accommodate climbing roses. Over two hundred varieties were planted representing shrub species, rugosa, hybrid rugosa, hybrid perpetual, moss, hybrid musk, damask, centifolia, Kordesii, and alba.

With a donation in 1992 from Thomas and Jane Nelson, the area was redesigned by the well-known landscape architect Michael van Valkenburgh and installed by Jim Robin. Features of the earlier garden were preserved—the Lundie-designed trellis, the circular layout, and the stone retaining walls modeled on the dry stone walls of Scotland. An elegant reflecting pool was placed in the center, and the garden was made handicapped-accessible.

New varieties were added during the renovation to emphasize a longer bloom period. Today the Shrub Rose Garden contains two groups of roses. The old garden roses are those that were in existence before the development of the first hybrid tea roses in 1867. The old roses—including the albas, centifolias, damasks, gallicas, and the moss roses—put on a spectacular bloom once a year. The second group, shrub roses, is a diverse mixture of plants both in their performance and in their ancestry. In general they are hardier and more disease-resistant than the hybrid teas. In addition, they re-bloom several times during the summer, in contrast to the old garden and species roses. In 2006 local sculptor Nick Legeros created a bronze of two children looking into the reflecting pool. This piece, commissioned by the Nelsons, whose generosity also continues to provide for the garden's consistent, high-quality maintenance, adds a fitting focal point to the central pool area.

THE MAZE GARDEN

The Arboretum's mission statement includes the call "to delight and inspire our visitors—with quality plants in well designed and maintained displays."[15] To that end the Arboretum has added two side-by-side mazes to its collection of gardens. Designed by William Frost and funded by numerous individuals, the mazes are nestled in the pine collection. Frost, who is a specialist in meditative garden designs, holds a Masters of Landscape Architecture degree from the University of Minnesota. The Arboretum's mazes have a diversity of plants (evergreen and deciduous), an informal layout with the path varying in width, and a series of surprising "nooks and crannies." One maze for younger visitors has crawl-through tunnels, and a more difficult maze awaits those a bit older. Bricks at the entry patio are

Built around an elegant reflecting pool, the Shrub Rose Garden features over two hundred varieties of shrub roses framed by stone retaining walls and Edwin Lundie-designed trellises.

inscribed with the names of donors who, intrigued by the concept of plants used for "garden fun," helped to fund the site's endowment.

MEYER-DEATS CONSERVATORY

On May 17, 1980, the Meyer-Deats Conservatory was dedicated, opening to warmth-starved Minnesotans the possibilities of year-round enjoyment of plant collections at the Arboretum. Dr. Edith Potter Deats, an internationally known perinatal pathologist, provided the generous gift which made the construction and development of the Conservatory possible. Dr. Deats was an avid horticulturist and an authority on tropical and subtropical plants, especially bromeliads. In memory of her two late husbands, she made a gift to showcase her passion for these exquisite plants.

At the glass entryway, the fragrance of jasmine (*Jasminium officianale*) and the blossoms of camellias greet the visitor. Along the sunny corridor, where temperatures are higher and moisture is lower, the cacti and succulents are clustered. Deeper in the main section, there are large and unusual tropicals and collections of bromeliads and orchids. Visitors can't miss the giant, white-flowered bird-of-paradise (*Strelitzia alba*) or its orange-blossomed sister (*Strelitzia reginae*). An enormous banana tree (*Musa*) and an equally statuesque weeping fig (*Ficus benjamina*) stand in the center.

To add contrast to the dominant green, there are numerous variegated plants such as the Chinese hibiscus (*Hibiscus rosa-sinensis* 'Variegata') and the frothy looking ficus (*Ficus benjamina* 'Variegata'). Uncommon plants are also featured—the ancient cycad (*Cycas circinalis*), commonly called the "dinosaur foot tree," and the Sago palm, which puts out a flush of brilliant green each year.

Clustered on display tables are a variety of orchids representing some of the world's thirty thousand species. The Conservatory aims to give some hint at this variety, but especially focuses on ones that do well in the home such as moth orchids (*Phalaenopsis*) and slipper orchids (*Phragmipedium* and *Paphiopedilum*)

which can flourish in low light and moisture levels.

The bromeliads, which are native to the Americas, are a much smaller family of about two thousand species. Their ability to take in moisture and nutrients through their leaves enables them to live in spots with little water like the sides of desert cacti or the tops of trees. The Conservatory has a representative sample of these plants, including those that thrive in a home setting such as the *Aechmea* 'Foster's Favorite' which has wine-red foliage and a dark-blue winter flower, followed

Side-by-side mazes, designed by William Frost, a specialist in meditative garden designs, contain a diversity of plants within surprising "nooks and crannies."

by red berries. Probably the best-known bromeliad here is *Aechmea fasciata* with its handsome silvery banded leaves and long-lived pink flower bract.

The Conservatory is a popular spot all year, but is a special favorite between November and March, drawing numerous visitors desiring a respite from Minnesota's monotonous palette of winter white.

THREE-MILE DRIVE

Three-Mile Drive is the main thoroughfare that winds through the Arboretum grounds. By tram, automobile, bus, bicycle, or on foot, visitors can take the paved road through rolling hills, native woodlands, prairies, collections and beautiful display gardens.

Early annual reports mention dusty roads and gravelling projects, but a 1969 Legislative grant enabled the Arboretum to pave all its roads, making the trek through the grounds much more enjoyable.

Unfortunately, by the 1990s Three-Mile Drive had become a "pothole" route. Subsequently, thanks to the generosity and commitment of Leonard and Mary Lou Hoeft and Leonard's many friends in the road-building industry, in 1993 the Drive was completely rebuilt. Leonard Hoeft brought together the paving, gravel, asphalt, and trucking industries to help, and in several weeks' time, they had removed the old road, filled the area with proper base material, and repaved the entire Drive. A "pothole" campaign brought in over $75,000, enough to cover most of the cost of services not donated.

In good or bad weather, walkers and riders have made

Three-Mile Drive one of the Arboretum's most popular destinations. Even to visitors who have no time to wander the gardens slowly, the Drive will give a sense of the Arboretum's extent and variety.

THE COLLECTIONS

In 1998 as part of the Arboretum's fortieth anniversary celebrations, plant curator Dave Stevenson made a summary of the Collections' history. Stevenson's words were published in the Arboretum newsletter:

A haven on cold, wintry days, the Meyer-Deats Conservatory overflows with tropical and sub-tropical plants.

As soon as the Arboretum was founded, the planting of collections began fast and furious. A number of plants went in the ground even before the Arboretum was actually dedicated in 1958.

From 1957 to 1965 the most extensive plantings, measured in numbers of species and cultivars and in numbers of plants, were apricots/cherries/plums, azaleas/rhododendrons, birch, crabapple, daylilies, dogwood, forsythia, hawthorn, honeysuckle, juniper, lilacs, lilies, maples, mockorange, pea shrubs, peonies, pine, potentilla, roses, viburnums, weigela, and yews.

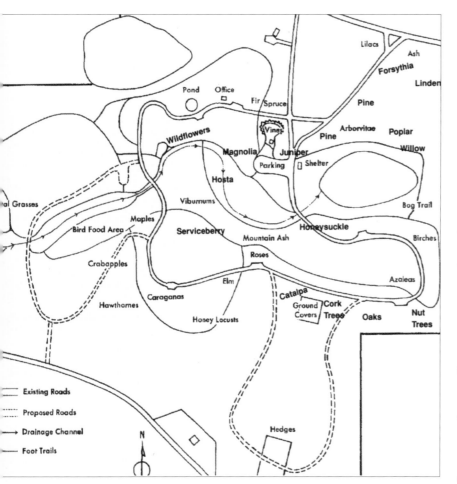

Taken from the 1998 Arboretum newsletter, this map shows the location of the collections in the early years of the Arboretum.

The adjacent map, modified from a 1965 brochure, shows the locations of collections at that time. It also shows the locations of proposed roads on newly acquired land; these match the current path of Three-Mile Drive. Several of the most extensive present-day Arboretum collections, crabapple, lilacs, and maples can be found on the map in their current location. . . . Other smaller but not necessarily less significant collections also are shown where you find them today: catalpa, oaks and nut, apricots/cherries/plums, serviceberry, mountain ash, elm. . . . Far and away the most numerous collections planted in this early period were rhododendrons and azaleas. This reflects the azalea breeding program that was initiated in 1955 at the Fruit Breeding Farm (now the Horticultural Research Center). Extensive plantings of species, cultivars and hybrids were needed to provide germplasm for the development of hardy azaleas. This program eventually produced the Northern Lights Series.[16]

Lilacs form the oldest plant collection. In 1960 a hedge of over two hundred Chinese lilacs was planted across the front of the Arboretum, parallel to the main road, and flanking the entrance were mass plantings of French hybrid lilacs. The design for the entrance planting was prepared by Leon C. Snyder, Jr., then a student in landscape architecture at Michigan State University, and noted local landscape architect Edmund Phelps.

When the entry was reconfigured, the Hella and Bill Hueg Lilac Collection was moved to a rise overlooking Alkire Drive, and in 1993 the Huegs sponsored a redesign. Landscape architect Jim Robin made the collection handicapped-accessible with a gently winding

The Arboretum maintains forty-eight collections, offering visitors the chance to compare trees and shrubs. The Linden Collection shows the variations in form and size of different species and cultivars of this genus.

Springtime brings out the glory of the Crabapple Collection, shown here framing the Winton Walkway. Crabapples are one of the most beautiful and useful small trees in the northern garden.

aggregate path. At the top is a circular resting area with a two-level stone wall, flagstone terrace, and benches. This small circle garden was given in memory of the Huegs' daughter, Anne Hueg Blackman (1956-1995). Large didactics explain the collection's history and give tips for the growing of lilacs.

ORNAMENTAL GRASSES

Dr. Mary Hockenberry Meyer created the Arboretum's collection of over two hundred ornamental and native grasses, one of the largest collections in North America, and she continues to oversee additions and changes to the plantings. There are fifty cultivars of Miscanthus ranging from 3½ inches to nearly twelve feet in height, eight cultivars of switch grass, and numerous other grasses and sedges. Meyer studies the plants for their usability in the region, focusing on winter interest, bloom time, growth habit, winter survival, and self-seeding.

With the renovation and enlargement of the display area in 2004, the garden was redesigned for greater visibility, access, and ease of comparison. All cultivars of any one grass were placed in straight rows where height and flower color can be observed, and didactic signs were erected to explain the uses and characteristics of each grass.

In 2004 Dr. Meyer's newly edited and updated publication, *Ornamental Grasses for Cold Climates*, was released by the Minnesota Extension Service. The book was the result of a six-year winter hardiness study of 165 ornamental grasses. Work done at the Arboretum and the University of Minnesota's Research and Outreach Centers in Crookston and Morris detailed the culture, maintenance, and landscape uses of the plants.

From her observations, Dr. Meyer discovered a new cultivar of little bluestem (*Schizachryium scoparium* 'Minnblue A') which she named 'Blue Heaven.' The grass is a striking plant with foliage ranging from dark blue and burgundy during the summer to red, purple and violet in the fall. It is taller and more upright than is typical, flowers in September, and carries its fall color into winter.

SPRING PEEPER MEADOW

Long ago, the area now called Spring Peeper Meadow was an opening in a dense forest, a sedge meadow with a rich, productive habitat. Hundreds of different plants and animals made their home here, and stands of maple and basswood ringed the basin. But in the mid-1800s, European settlers began to farm the land, cutting trees and planting crops. Eventually they used tiles to drain away the water in order to farm the fertile soil beneath.

By the 1990s the thirty-acre site currently on the Arboretum's eastern edge was targeted for residential and light-industrial development. The proposed development with its hard surface runoff from roads, roofs, and parking lots threatened to have a negative impact on the Arboretum's research plots and collections. Peter Olin, Arboretum director, established a land planning committee and conducted a site analysis to determine Arboretum watershed boundaries. The information gathered indicated that the Arboretum needed to acquire the area to protect its watershed.

Proposals for funding were developed and sent to the

The Hueg Lilac Collection was redesigned in 1993 to include a handicapped-accessible path, stone wall, and flagstone terrace. Signage explains the collection's history and give tips for growing lilacs.

The Ornamental Grass Collection is one of the largest such collections in North America and provides visitors an opportunity to observe and select appropriate grasses for the home garden.

LCMR (Legislative Commission on Minnesota Resources) and the Minnehaha Creek Watershed District. The proposals asked for funds to purchase the acreage and to re-establish the sedge meadow wetland. When funding from these sources was matched with private monies, the land was acquired and the project begun. Mary Lee and Wallace Dayton began an endowment.

Dr. Susan Galatowitsch, ecologist and University of Minnesota professor, became project coordinator and started the complex task of restoration in 1995. The site preparation, which took eighteen months,

was made especially difficult because of the dense cover of reed canary grass (*Phalaris arundinacea*) still commonly used by farmers to stabilize poor soil but recently considered a major invasive species. Once the reed canary grass was removed, the drain tiles were broken allowing the basin to refill with water. Reseeding and replanting followed using both seeds collected regionally and those purchased commercially as well as plants grown from the collected seed.

One hundred and twelve species were introduced to the wetland as crews planted over sixty thousand seedlings and transplants of sedge meadow plants at Spring Peeper. Fred Rozumalski, a landscape architect, designed a 450-foot boardwalk that crosses the water, allowing school children and other visitors access to the wetland. Interpretive signs interspersed along the path and boardwalk explain the meadow's history and restoration.

In addition, volunteers and staff planted five thousand seedlings of maple, basswood, and other native trees and shrubs on the slopes above the sedge meadow and prairie. In the spring of 1999, a Department of Natural Resources grant obtained by research fellow Julia Bohnen funded this reforestation project.

At present, the boardwalk zigzags across the wetland, trails encircle it, and the Gallistel Overlook, funded by Audrey and Albert Gallistel, sits on a high point. All provide opportunities to observe at close range the plants now in the meadow including nineteen species

The Collections

ARALIA, ARBORVITAE, ASH, BIRCH (NEW), BIRCH (OLD), BUCKEYE, CATALPA, CORKTREE, CRABAPPLE, CURRANT/DEUTZIA, DAYLILY/MUM, DWARF CONIFER, ELM, FIR, HAWTHORN, HEDGE, HONEYLOCUST (LEGUMES), HYDRANGEA, LARCH (NEW), LARCH (OLD), LILAC, LINDEN, MAGNOLIA, MAPLE, MISCELLANEOUS SHRUB, MOUNTAIN ASH, MOCK ORANGE, OAK AND NUT, OLD ASH, ORNAMENTAL GRASS, PEA SHRUB, PINE, POPLAR, POTENTILLA, PRUNUS, SERVICEBERRY, SMALL TREE, SPIREA, SPRUCE, SUMAC/ SMOKETREE, UPRIGHT TREES, VIBURNUM, WEEPING TREE, WEIGELA, WILLOW

The Spring Peeper Meadow, once cut-over farmland, is being restored to the sedge meadow it once was. The restoration has been very successful and has made possible the return of many plants and animals. Here, it is seen in the green of spring (top) and in the hazy colors of fall.

of sedges, several grasses, and numerous wildflowers. Animals also abound in the area. Visitors can see muskrat lodges, and more than ninety-five bird species have been sighted in and around the meadow including lesser yellowlegs and common yellowthroats, both of which inhabit wetlands. Shy Virginia rails and the secretive sedge wrens have also been spotted.

Both Olin and Galatowitsch agree that this restoration is unique. "In wetland restoration, usually people just let the water come back into the area," explained Galatowitsch. "A sedge meadow has never been fully restored before. One of our goals is to recreate wetlands with high botanical interest. Of the 112 species planted, we've observed some 65 percent remaining. This rate of establishment is far greater than the 25 to 35 percent establishment rate attained in other restorations."[17]

PARKING LOT SOLUTIONS

Not just a place to showcase beautiful plants, the Arboretum is an institution that is intent on demonstrating environmentally solid practices. As part of that mission, it has planned its three major parking lots with systems to improve the environment in several ways. When Peter Olin became Arboretum director, he brought his landscape architecture background into play. "I thought the Arboretum parking lots should give guidance to those who build and use them and also be environmentally friendly," Olin explained.[18] Goals include modifying polluted rainfall runoff, showcasing attractive alternative screening plants, and reducing heat build-up. In addition, these

lots demonstrate the cost effectiveness of good design and ways to help compensate for the problems caused by urbanization.

The first parking area built was the main visitor Parking Court, designed by landscape architect Barry Warner and completed in 1991. Here the double wide bays were planted in four different ways: with native and drought-resistant plants, with trees and shrubs, with flowering and fragrant plants, and with evergreens and plants for winter interest. Fred Rozumalski, then a student in Landscape Architecture at the University of Minnesota, selected the plant material, choosing species that were hardy and salt-tolerant. Many, like the common hackberry and trembling aspen, also provide shade. All can withstand the tough growing conditions that parking lots create, yet most are not commonly used in parking lot plantings. The rich mixture of trees, shrubs, and flowering plants provides more visual interest than is usually seen in parking lots, while at the same time helping to screen views and reduce noise and heat levels.

In 2003, additional parking spaces were needed, and the Arboretum hired Sherri Buss, a landscape ecologist with Bonestroo, Rosene, Anderlik and Associates, to design rain gardens to collect surface runoff.

Traditionally rainwater is drained away from parking lots through pipes going directly into storm water systems. In a rain garden, the lot is sloped and built without curbs. Here, the rain or snowmelt travels across the lot, collecting oil, gasoline, and other pollutants on its way to the gardens.

The Arboretum's rain gardens are constructed of two feet of sand and six inches of sandy loam. Each is thirty feet wide and ranges from sixty to two hundred feet in length. The plants are mostly natives that can withstand drought since the swale is dry most of the time. Trees like bur oak (*Quercus macrocarpa*), swamp white oak (*Quercus bicolor*), Amur maackia (*Maackia amurensis*); shrubs like arctic blue willow (*Salix purpurea* 'Nana') and bush honeysuckle (*Diervilla lonicera*); and thirty kinds of perennial flowers and grasses soak up the rain water while filtering the pollutants.

This system aids in replenishing groundwater by removing pollutants via plants and soils. It also helps to stop erosion and habitat destruction near wetlands, creeks and other bodies of water. The Arboretum hopes that the rainwater gardens will show developers and public officials that such gardens are effective in areas where large amounts of rainwater accumulate.

The third parking lot, for the Andrus Learning Center, was also constructed in 2003. Designed by landscape architect Jim Robin and sponsored by the Minnehaha Creek Watershed District with help from the Metropolitan Council, this experimental space utilizes five equal-sized collection basins, each using a different pavement and planting technique. They range from totally permeable paving surrounded by shrubs (Watershed No. 1) to no plantings and totally impermeable paving material (Watershed No. 5). The parking lot is sloped so that all rain and snow melt drains into the watershed pools. Watershed No. 5 exhibits nearly 100 percent runoff; Watershed No. 1 has nearly 100 percent absorption.

All the parking lot experiments demonstrate ways to maintain clean wetlands and rivers and to reduce urban flooding. They provide models for professionals and homeowners to compare the appearance and effectiveness of different treatments of storm water runoff.

Director Peter Olin has focused attention on parking lots, making those at the Arboretum models of environmentally sound practices. This run-off parking lot demonstrates paving ranging in degrees of permeability and density of plantings.

DEPARTMENTS and PROGRAMS

CHAPTER FIVE

EDUCATION

When conceived, the Arboretum had the dual emphases of research and education, one major aim being to encourage Minnesota citizens' interest in horticulture and plant science. In outlining its objectives in 1960, the Arboretum's annual report stated that this was to be a place to "distribute knowledge concerning the plants being grown (here) through tours in the arboretum, garden talks by staff members, newspaper and magazine articles, and through arboretum publications."[1]

In one sense, even a casual visit to the Arboretum has an educational component. Plants are labeled, gardens are organized, and interpretive signs provide facts—all enabling visitors to easily absorb information about the natural world as they meander through the grounds. Over the years, a diverse and targeted educational endeavor has evolved in response to the goal stated at the Arboretum's inception, and what began modestly has become a multi-faceted program reaching hundreds of adults, young people, and children every year.

In 1999 Dr. Emily Hoover became Director of Education. A prominent teacher in the Department of Horticultural Science at the University of Minnesota, Dr. Hoover has received the University's top teaching award and the USDA's Teaching Excellence Award, given to only eight people nationally each year.

Adults can take classes year-round on an enormous

range of topics. They can participate in extended workshops and conferences on the environment and horticulture. Children also can join campus activities such as day camps, the fourteen-week Children's Garden, or one-day explorations at the Marion Andrus Learning Center and the Sally Pegues Oswald Growing Place for Kids. With their parents and grandparents, they can plant seeds, make crafts, or experiment with ecology. School groups visit daily during the fall, winter, and spring. Through the Plantmobile, children who cannot attend the Arboretum classes are able to study plant science in school, and at several inner city sites, young people have a chance to learn about gardening by

Planting seeds of one's own: thousands of plants go home yearly with students on fieldtrips.

Matt Schuth, wildlife expert, shows a puffball (a type of fungus often found in the woods) to a group of hikers.

raising vegetables and flowers. In day-long workshops and graduate courses, teachers study the myriad ways in which plants can bring life to the classroom. People with special needs can also expand their experiences and knowledge with planting projects and crafts.

In addition, each year through the Volunteer Coordinator's office, hundreds of volunteers are given basic training before being stationed at jobs throughout the Arboretum.

This enormous expansion, which continues to the present, shows the great vision demonstrated by leadership, staff members and benefactors over the years of the Arboretum's operation.

In the early days, with no indoor facilities, guided tours

were the prime educational forum, and annual reports listed the number and types of groups in attendance. The report of 1963 noted that 160 organized study groups had come that year including garden clubs, church groups, youth clubs, and school groups, and the annual reports have proudly noted increased attendance every year since then.

With the greater demands, the staff began to feel the need for indoor classroom space. In 1968 the machine shed was converted into a classroom which could accommodate groups of one hundred. The staff, principally Mervin Eisel, extension horticulturist, and Dr. Harold Pellett, horticulture professor, began a well-attended series of spring classes. For one dollar, Arboretum members could study a variety of topics including "Wildflowers for the Garden" or "Pruning Deciduous Ornamentals." (Non-members paid two dollars.) Tours continued on Saturdays with classes on the gathering and processing of maple syrup being especially popular.

In 1969, the Arboretum made a grand summary of its greatly expanded educational activities. There had been 388 tours for almost 11,000 individuals and gardening classes for 700 participants. School groups were becoming a large part of the schedule. Elementary students numbered 6,738; junior and senior high school students numbered 469.

Staff realized that the converted shed was simply a stop-gap measure. Needed was a large indoor facility to accommodate offices, classroom space, a library, and research. In response, the Board announced plans in 1967 for an Education and Research Building and started an ambitious fund-raising process.

To design the building, the Arboretum hired noted architect Edwin Lundie who had set his stamp on the grounds earlier with the well-house, entrance design, Ordway Shelter, and trellises for the vine collection.

Construction was begun in 1971, and in 1974 the handsome Leon C. Snyder Education and Research Building was opened to the public. Here, in addition to offices, a tea room, and a library, were three classrooms which could each accommodate about forty to fifty people and an auditorium with seating for one hundred fifty.

With the expanded classroom space, curriculum offerings grew. Staff members, including Dr. Snyder, Mike Zins, extension horticulturist, and Jane McKinnon, professor of Horticultural Science, taught hundreds of enthusiastic adults in daytime and evening sessions, both spring and fall, on topics ranging from "Beginning Bonsai" to "Growing Vegetables." In addition, numerous tours were offered for children. Schools often used this opportunity to give students first-hand experience in ecology, plant science, or horticulture. By 1977, the annual report noted that 12 percent of all those attending the Arboretum were involved in some type of educational programming.

In 1978, Arboretum director Dr. Francis de Vos presented an in-depth study to the Arboretum Auxiliary, proposing a children's program. An adequate one for children was lacking, he noted, citing thriving programs in other botanical gardens and arboreta. The Auxiliary presented de Vos with a check for $3,500

Elmer Andersen, Dr. Leon C. Snyder, John E. P. Morgan, and Edwin Lundie pose by the Ordway Shelter as they prepare for the ground-breaking of the Snyder Education Building.

and a commitment of $5,000 more in 1979.

Named the Growing Place and coordinated by Sandy Tanck, a graduate student in horticulture at the University of Minnesota, the program opened in 1979. Here elementary age children could learn about the world of plants through role-playing, gardening activities, and games. Topics were selected to complement the science curriculum used in Minnesota schools.

The following year a Children's Garden was added. This session ran from May through August and provided children ages eight to twelve with the opportunity to grow vegetables, herbs, and flowers. A giant Harvest Festival in August capped off the summer's accomplishments. In writing about the program, Tanck summarized, "From the viewpoint of the staff more than vegetables are under cultivation in the summer session.

Horticulturist and long-time staff member Merv Eisel led many groups
through the Arboretum, such as this group of school children from the 1950s.

Our purpose is to provide the child with a successful experience in managing his or her own piece of borrowed earth. . . . Each garden plot is a miniature piece of nature, created by two young partners who are responsible for its management."[2]

In 1993 the American Association of Botanic Gardens and Arboreta recognized the Youth Education Program, directed by Tanck, with its AABGA Award for Program Excellence. In handing out this prestigious award, the Committee Chair, Dr. Richard W. Lightly, said, "I have never reviewed an educational program so carefully grounded and developed as this one."[3]

The award was an acknowledgement of all that Tanck and her staff had accomplished. Classes and activities had increased, reaching twenty-four thousand students a year. There were greenhouse and orchard classes. The Plantmobile, funded by Marilyn Erickson, traveled daily to classrooms through the Twin Cities and surrounding rural areas. Most importantly, a new building had been added, the Learning Center, dedicated on June 3, 1983. At its opening, Tanck recognized the contributions of the major donors, Marion and John Andrus III and the Donald T. Knutson family: "Their enthusiasm for our mission—the education of children—has been an enormous boon to us through the years."[4]

The education facility added a hands-on dimension to the program. Here, children had easy access to microscopes, a greenhouse, pots and seeds, a talking tree, and of course, gardens. The active, experiential approach to learning, from plant propagation to terrarium construction, ensured the program's popularity.

And once again, the new space facilitated new growth. More children and their families came through the doors each year. By the late 1990s, the four-thousand-square-foot center was full to bursting. In response, the

The excitement of nature comes alive for children when they study plants at close hand.

building was completely remodeled and a new wing added. In 2001, when completed, the Center had tripled in size. The new wing was named the Sally Pegues Oswald Growing Place for Kids, funded by Charles Oswald in memory of his wife. The original building was renamed the Marion Andrus Learning Center in recognition of the Andrus family's contribution and in memory of Marion Andrus.

Tim Kenny joined the staff in 1992 as an instructor with a focus on urban gardening. At the beginning there were two inner city sites, each with twenty children participating. These eight-week programs had a science-based, hands-on approach. Youngsters, aged five to ten, planted, tended and harvested vegetables, all the while playing games which incorporated a learning component. By 2006 other sites had been added, two in Minneapolis and one in St. Paul, and ten instructors were reaching 150 children during the summer.

In 1995 Kenny started a program for urban teens. This one, named by the participants as CityFresh, targeted youth who were too old for the Children's Garden but

With the aid of microscopes, youngsters can observe the intricate workings of plants.

The fragrance and color of spring comes early in the warmth of the "Please Touch" greenhouse where students are invited to touch, smell, draw, and discover plants "up-close."

still interested in aspects of horticulture. Teens in CityFresh take an entrepreneurial approach to plants. Each summer they determine projects for the season, decide on a product, research the market, develop the product, and sell it. In the process they learn work and social skills along with math and marketing. An adult leader with interest and expertise in some aspect of horticulture works with each group. Small groups have focused on garden photography, land-scape design and installation, and raising specialty produce for sale to local restaurants.

Kenny sees the urban outreach—both the Children's Gardens and CityFresh—"as an equity issue. This is so necessary," he said. "Affluent kids have access to nature, to gardening, to classes about the environment. Many inner-city kids do not. This helps right that imbalance."[5]

ADULT EDUCATION

Programming for adults has grown apace with that for children. At first a small schedule of classes was added to the tours, and with the growth of the Arboretum facilities, these classes began to be offered year-round, increased in number, and became more ambitious in scope. By 2007 adult learners could participate in a wide range of hour-long to weekend-long classes including symposia for professionals as well as amateurs.

Shirley Mah Kooyman became Adult Education Manager in 1993 and has brought in noted speakers from the U.S. and abroad. She has also set up partnerships with groups, such as the Minnesota State Horticultural Society and the Minnesota Extension Service, to co-sponsor workshops on a vast array of horticultural and environmental topics.

In 1992 Director Peter Olin, assisted by Kooyman, started a series of seminars called the Parking Lot Conferences, inviting in people from around the country to give thought to dealing with one of the Arboretum's

People of all ages take advantage of educational opportunities, both formal and informal.

most daunting environmental challenges. After several years Kooyman, Olin, and Colston Burrell, then plant curator, established the Art of Specialty Gardens series which became a spring tradition for area gardeners. Here plant enthusiasts learned gardening basics as well as gained information on sophisticated design and plant topics. Later, conferences on issues of public policy, such as sustainable agriculture and water resources management, were added to the education offerings, and by 2006 the schedule featured 120 choices. Through these classes, taught on site as well as at distant venues, participants of varied backgrounds and interests can learn to cook, paint, write, and meditate, as well as plant and prune.

Kooyman stated that the thrust of the education program is "to educate the public on a bit of the science relating to horticulture, botany, natural science, and garden design. Because of our unique setting, the gardens are outdoor classrooms, where students can get up close and smell the roses."[6]

In 2005 Kooyman started the Arboretum Gardening School which offers its own series of classes. The curriculum covers the full range of gardening topics, arranged seasonally and taught by Kooyman and other experts in the field. Participants who complete all twenty-four topics receive a letter of completion. Industry professionals as well as amateurs have taken advantage of the well-organized offerings.

A series of free, drop-in classes utilize the Keating Greenhouse in the Home Demonstration Gardens. These Saturday, hands-on classes include a repotting

clinic and a propagation workshop.

The Education Department also trains tour volunteers, a program Kooyman initiated in 1987. From April through October, trainees meet with Kooyman for forty hours of class work. Sessions include Arboretum history, garden design, botany, and the layout of the Arboretum. The training prepares guides to lead bus and walking tours, and to drive and narrate the Trumpet Creeper Tram tours.

Since its earliest years, the Arboretum has sponsored travel tours throughout the United States and abroad. By 2006-07 there were six yearly tours to such destinations as the California wine country, Santa Fe and Taos, Japan, and Thailand, led by the director and other members of the staff.

THERAPEUTIC HORTICULTURE

Through the ages, the importance of horticulture to the healing process has been recognized. In the late 1980s Director Peter Olin organized a committee to explore the possibility of adding a horticultural therapy program. After visiting the Chicago Botanic Garden and its unique sensory garden and Horticultural Therapy program, he envisioned doing something similar at the Arboretum. After much discussion, he hired Katherine McFadden, then a landscape architecture graduate student, to plan out such a curriculum and subsequently appointed Jean Larson to coordinate it.

The goal was to provide opportunities for using plants, horticulture, and other nature-based activities to enrich the lives of individuals struggling with chemical dependency, eating disorders, and physical and mental difficulties, as

Jean Larson, coordinator of the Therapeutic Horticulture Program, works with many populations—those with physical or mental difficulties, advancing age, chemical dependency, and eating disorders. In caring for plants, participants report benefits in social and cognitive skills, rehabilitation, and physical adaptation.

The fully accessible Clotilde Irvine Sensory Garden reflects many of the Arboretum's gardens and collections.

well as the challenges associated with advancing age; and in 1992, coordinator Jean Larson noted benefits for the participants in four basic areas: cognition skill building, social improvement, psychological development, and physical adaptation and rehabilitation.

In collaboration with various service agencies such as hospitals, prisons, and group homes, the Arboretum helps design and implement programs for their clientele, teaching social service professionals to use horticulture as a therapeutic tool at their own institutions. Long-time collaborations have existed with Choice Programs for adults with developmental disabilities; Sojourners, a day program for the elderly; Dakota Communities, an umbrella organization for group homes; and the Struthers Parkinson's Center at Methodist Hospital. In addition, the program provides

activities and workshops for individuals with special needs on the Arboretum grounds as well as off-site, and by 2006, thirty-two thousand people with diverse needs had taken part.

Larson has also brought an international component to therapeutic horticulture at the Arboretum. In 1995 in Israel at the International Federation on Aging's Global Conference, she made a presentation on a three-year intergenerational program connecting children and the frail elderly. In 2006 Larson and fellow Arboretum staff member Mary Meyer published the *Sourcebook for Intergenerational Therapeutic Horticulture: Bringing Elders and Children Together*, which presents a hands-on, easy-to-use activity plan that benefits the development of relationships between the elderly and school-age children.

In 1998 Larson spent sixteen weeks in northern Japan as a consultant to Towa Town's nursing home and returned again the following year as a consultant. Her third visit to Japan was spent traveling throughout the country teaching workshops and training staff at a variety of nursing homes and other health care facilities in the therapeutic uses of horticulture. In 2000 and 2003, Larson spent a month in England and Sweden learning about horticulture therapy programs in those countries. In addition, social service professionals from abroad have come to the Arboretum to study under her tutelage. Most recently, Larson gave a lecture presentation at Oxford University for the International Congress on Education in Botanic Gardens.

Dedicated on July 1, 1996, the Clotilde Irvine Sensory Garden and Therapeutic Horticulture Center brought new dimensions to the scope of the Arboretum. In this fully accessible garden where persons with and without physical and mental challenges can interact, visitors can see, smell, touch, hear, and occasionally taste the delights of the natural world, participating in hands-on activities and observing accessible garden design and containers.

In cooperation with various organizations, the Therapeutic Horticultural Center sponsors a bi-yearly lecture series which has featured authors, architects, and health-care professionals.

In 2004 the American Horticulture Therapy Association gave official recognition to a series of courses that Jean Larson and her staff had devised. There are five University of Minnesota courses, taught by the Department of Horticultural Science and others, offered through the University's Center for Spirituality and Healing. These provide students the opportunity to learn specialized skills in the field of therapeutic horticulture. On completion of the fifteen-credit course work, students receive a Therapeutic Horticulture Certificate which gives points toward registering as a horticultural therapist.

Larson defined the benefits of the Arboretum's Therapeutic Programs as three-fold: "They create public awareness of therapeutic horticulture and of those with special needs. They provide a healing benefit directly to those who are served. Perhaps most importantly they create a ripple effect; as more people are trained, they take the information out into their communities."[7] And in 2004, the Minnesota State Horticulture Society presented her with the Distinguished Service Award in recognition of the work she had done with the Center for Therapeutic Horticulture.

HORTICULTURAL RESEARCH CENTER

Through the century of its existence, the Horticultural Research Center has changed its focus in response to changing agricultural realities. In 1908 when it began as the Fruit Breeding Farm, most Minnesotans lived on farms and relied on their own home-grown fruits and vegetables. Many were attempting to grow fruit which they had brought with them from Europe or the East Coast, but Minnesota's climate proved too harsh for most of these varieties. The Fruit Breeding Farm concentrated on developing an apple hardy enough for our cold climate. Other crops of importance were grapes, plums, raspberries, apricots and strawberries.

At the time, almost every state had its own breeding

program to develop locally adapted fruit; however, because of the expense involved and the long breeding cycle, few states have continued their efforts in this area. The program at the University of Minnesota is the last major one in the Midwest, and so Minnesota's recent introductions have attracted interest both from other states and other countries.

Now that most Minnesotans purchase their fruit at the local grocery store, the HRC has shifted its major concentration from home growers to commercial ones, and its recent introductions of apples, grapes, and blueberries are being grown across the United States, South America, Europe, and southern Canada. These introductions are usually suitable for home growers also and so in addition, the HRC continues research useful for the individual gardener on apricots, crabapples, and pears.

Minnesota's severe climate also limited the choice of "ornamentals," those plants grown for beauty and landscape development, not for eating. Lovely plants grown elsewhere, such as azaleas, could not survive the state's cold winters. To ameliorate this situation, the Woody Landscape Breeding and Genetics Program

The early blooms of the Anise Magnolia (*Magnolia Salicifolia*) brighten the walk in the shade tree exhibit.

was formally initiated, and its work was added to that of the Fruit Breeding Farm in 1954. In 1967 the Farm's name was changed to the Horticultural Research Center to reflect its broader mission, and in 1987 the HRC became part of the Arboretum, its central focus remaining the goal of developing hardy

plants that will thrive in the challenging climate of Minnesota and other northern sites.

On the combined acreage of the Arboretum and the HRC, researchers study the breeding, growth, and propagation of woody plants, especially shrub roses,

At the Horticultural Research Center (HRC), the renovation and additions to the main building greatly improved the opportunities for research and development. Labs were updated, office and storage spaces were expanded, and a wine research area was added. The project was completed and dedication (shown here) took place in 2000.

NORTHERN TREASURE

azaleas, rhododendrons, and red maples. They develop methods for restoring prairies and wetlands, and they breed and evaluate ornamental grasses. In addition, they develop high quality fruit, appraising various species for disease resistance, vigor, taste, and winter hardiness. With its diverse landscape of wetlands, prairie, and gently rolling hills, added to its situation between suburb and farmland, the HRC is well suited for the study of plant performance. In its one hundred year history, the 230-acre Horticultural Research Center has been a boon to the nursery and fruit growing industries, generating more than 130 introductions. Many of these are nationally known and still in demand.

The improvement and enlargement of HRC facilities have enabled researchers to expand their work. The Center's first greenhouse was built over sixty years ago as part of a WPA project. Many fine introductions, including the Honeycrisp™ apple and the Lights azaleas, came from this building. However, by 1980 the greenhouse was becoming unusable.

In 1981, through the efforts of Horticultural Science Department head, Dr. Jim Bartz, the Minnesota legislature funded a greatly modernized greenhouse. Though not much larger than the original one, the new greenhouse has an open design and three sections allowing different temperatures for varying experiments.

Also showing its age was the stucco "600 Building"— home to HRC offices, labs, and workspace. Arboretum director Peter Olin observed that the situation had become more than uncomfortable. "Research projects have been constrained for years because of the old facilities,"

Olin said.[8] Again, through another Department of Horticultural Science head, Dr. Gary Gardner, the Legislature funded an addition to and renovation of the "600 Building."

At the same time, the need was recognized for a wine research facility and the hiring of an enologist (wine specialist). The wine research center and "600 Building" renovation were combined into one project, and by the spring of 2000, construction was completed. In the new building there were meeting rooms, office space for scientists and support staff, spacious laboratories, and improved capacity for storing apples from the breeding projects. Equipment was brought up to date and climate controls were installed. The new facility had an impact beyond increased comfort. Productivity also improved with the additional space and the capacity to work on a greater number of products at one time.

FRUIT

As director of the Fruit Breeding Program, Professor James Luby supervises research on various fruits. Currently research is focused on apples, blueberries, strawberries, and wine and table grapes, with a smaller effort on apricots, pears, cherries, currants, and crabapples for the home landscape.

The Minnesota fruit-growing industry is highly dependent on varieties introduced at the HRC. All blueberry production and a majority of the raspberry production are based on varieties introduced by the University or those directly descended from them. In the state's commercial vineyards and wineries, over half of the grapes grown are varieties developed at the HRC, and two-thirds of the apple varieties grown commercially

Dave Bedford, the Research Center's chief apple breeder, helped discover the popular Honeycrisp™ apple.

were developed at the Center. In addition to the Honeycrisp™ apple, currently the most widely planted variety in the state, and Zestar!™, a recent introduction, some of the older varieties still widely grown include 'Beacon,' 'Prairie Spy,' 'Fireside,' and 'Haralson,' Minnesota's all-time favorite.

Today's breeders use many of the labor-intensive techniques employed by the early fruit breeders such as hybridizing the best parents and selecting the most promising offspring. Fortunately, however, several innovations have helped to speed up the process. For example, laboratory freezing tests help select the hardiest specimens without waiting for the occasional "test" winter, the use of dwarfing rootstock reduces the space and time needed to bring the thousands of seedlings to the fruiting stage, and tissue culture propagation provides a way to reproduce large numbers of disease-free fruit at once. These techniques expedite the process of getting trees to fruit growers and local nurseries.

APPLES

Breeders are patient people. They have to be because it takes decades to discover and bring to market a new plant. In fact, for apples the process usually takes about thirty years. Of the fifteen thousand trees growing at the Research Center at any time, only one will be named and released to the market. Fortunately, every now and then, a fantastic fruit will come along that makes the wait worthwhile.

For scientist David Bedford, the Center's chief apple breeder, that fruit was Honeycrisp™. When Bedford arrived at the HRC in 1979, among the many apples he evaluated was MN1711 (later named Honeycrisp™)—a variety that had been growing almost twenty years and already been tagged "discard" by previous evaluators. Bedford noted, however, that the MN1711 samples were growing in the worst site, one which was low and damp—conditions which had resulted in 80 percent of the trees in that area dying due to a difficult winter. Bedford decided to remove the "discard" tag and give the tree another chance.

In the 1980s, Luby and Bedford tasted the MN1711 apples again. During tasting season, scientists taste hundreds of apples a day, but the two knew immediately this was something special—it was attractive, sweet-tart, and had an explosively crisp texture described by one grower as a "one-of-a-kind crispness that no previous apple had ever possessed."[9] They decided to send this one to the public, and in 1991 Honeycrisp™ was given its name and released to growers.

Most apple varieties introduced by the University over the decades have been primarily limited in popularity to this region. Not so Honeycrisp™. The apple was quickly adopted by growers in all the major apple-producing regions in the country from the state of Washington to New England. A bit later Europe, Australia, South Africa, and New Zealand began growing Honeycrisp™, and by 2008 there were over five million Honeycrisp™ trees in cultivation.

The University of Minnesota's development of the Honeycrisp™ apple was honored as one of the top twenty-five innovations in the last decade by the *2006 Better World Report*, a publication which recog-nizes significant academic research and technology transfers that have changed our way of life and made the world a better place. The award puts the HRC's contributions on the same level of importance as medical discoveries such as the cochlear implant and

The chronology of getting an apple to market.

Compiled by Dr. James Luby

SPRING, YEAR 1: Pollen is selected from two parent plants, a cross is made by hand, and the fruit is allowed to mature.

FALL, YEAR 2: Apples from the controlled crosses are harvested and the seed collected.

YEAR 3: Seeds are planted in the greenhouse.

YEAR 4: The new trees are grafted onto rootstock and field planted. Over the next few years, they are regularly inspected for disease and cold damage.

YEAR 7-YEAR 22: The trees start bearing fruit and are extensively tested for hardiness, disease resistance, and fruit quality. More than 99 percent of the original crosses are eliminated.

YEAR 22-YEAR 23: Initial field propagation is undertaken by nurseries to create enough stock to make available for sale.

YEAR 27: Substantial stock is available to apple growers and home gardeners.

YEAR 32: First significant amount of fruit is available in markets.

In spring, rows upon rows of apple trees burst into bloom at the Horticultural Research Center.

technological innovations such as Google.

In 2006, following the 1998 introduction of the Zestar!™ apple—an early season variety with a sweet-tart crunch—Bedford and Luby released SnowSweet™ which has a rich, sweet flavor and snow-white flesh. Now the two scientists are looking at niche markets. "There is an enormous range with apples, "Bedford explained. "They can be tiny little things or quite large. They can taste of chocolate or cherries. What we see in the grocery store is just a small band of what exists. Our philosophy isn't to get another Honeycrisp™ or 'Red Delicious,' but to think outside the box."[10]

GRAPES

The Horticultural Research Center has been at work developing high-quality, cold-hardy grapes for over a century. The Depression of the 1930s and World War II interrupted the work, but in the last two decades grape breeding has again become a major focus for the Center.

The one-hundred-strong membership of the Minnesota Grape Growers Association had lobbied the Legislature for money to develop hardy cultivars that would not require labor-intensive vineyard care, and the current program began in earnest with the passage in 1984 of a bill to appropriate funds specifically for grape research. With these dollars, scientist Peter Hemstad, a viticulturist, was hired to work full-time on grape breeding activities.

In 2000, the well-equipped enology laboratory and research winery were completed, enabling Hemstad and enologist Anna Katharine Mansfield to better produce and evaluate grapes and wine. Though there are other grape breeding programs in the United States, only the HRC is working to develop grapes hardy to thirty to forty degrees below zero.

The Center's vineyard of approximately ten thousand vines is planted on eleven acres. Each year over one thousand vines are planted and tested, with a similar amount being culled out. These vines have a diverse genetic base. Most include *Vitis riparia* (river grape), Minnesota's wild species, for its cold-hardy nature. To this is added *Vitis vinifera*, the traditional European wine grape, with its high-quality, wine-producing traits. Every year over one hundred University of Minnesota advanced selections and over four hundred cultivars and selections from other breeders are under evaluation. They must demonstrate cold-hardiness and disease resistance, but equally important qualities are taste, productivity, growth habit, bud break, and ripening times. In addition, the HRC prepares about one hundred wines every year, looking for grapes with superior winemaking potential. Enologist Mansfield has supervised the winemaking process since 2000. Her staff is able to make wines under exacting protocols from even the smallest quantities that might come from a single vine, and the quality of these "micro-vinifications" can determine whether an experimental selection will be introduced as a new variety or summarily culled from the vineyard.

From this program have come four introductions: 'Frontenac' (1996), 'LaCrescent' (2002), 'Frontenac gris' (2003), and 'Marquette' (2006). The four represent red, white, rose, and dessert wines and have been adopted by regional wineries. From the first planting to the discovery of a variety worthy of naming and releasing takes about fifteen years. "About one of every ten thousand seedlings has all the qualities necessary to become a named variety," Hemstad explained.[11]

WOODY LANDSCAPE PLANTS

The University of Minnesota has long had the reputation as one of the finest research facilities in the world for breeding and selecting cold-hardy woody landscape plants and for developing new production and protection methods. The program has been responsible for the release of forty-seven woody landscape plants which have greatly expanded the palette of landscape plant material available in the upper Midwest. Introductions have included flowering trees, shrubs, large shade trees, roses and deciduous azaleas.

In 2001 Dr. Stan Hokanson became director of the Woody Landscape Plant Breeding Program, succeeding Harold Pellett. He has continued work with deciduous azaleas, looking for those which resist powdery mildew and those which will flower in July or August. In addition, he has initiated new avenues of research.

One major thrust has been research with evergreen rhododendrons. Hokanson, along with Arboretum Director Olin, secured funding and installed a new rhododendron display and evaluation garden on the Arboretum's Three-Mile Drive. The site is planted with cultivars that have been maintained at the Arboretum for several years as well as new selections and cultivars from breeding projects in this country and around the world. The rhododendron garden is unique—there are no other public display gardens of evergreen rhododendrons in Zone 4 of the United States, and plants that show superior traits will be used as parents in a breeding program for hardy evergreen rhododendrons.

Aware of the enormous genetic potential available in the diverse native environment of the region, Hokanson and fellow scientists have begun collecting and appraising indigenous plants. Their research has resulted in the identification of several small trees, shrubs, and ground covers which have demonstrated many desirable traits useful in hybridizing to develop good landscape plants.

ANDERSEN HORTICULTURAL LIBRARY

Like all institutions, Andersen Horticultural Library started as an idea. Anticipating the new educational building, Leon Snyder conceived of a library as a necessary part of that structure. The library was to serve the Arboretum staff, the University of Minnesota faculty and students, and the general public. Former governor Elmer L. Andersen and his wife Eleanor, already supportive of the Arboretum, promised their support in funding the library, along with its books and furnishings, and the hiring of a librarian.

In 1969, June Rogier, a University librarian but also an Arboretum volunteer, was chosen to select, purchase, and process books for the new facility. The library was to be called the Elmer L. and Eleanor J. Andersen Horticultural Library in honor of its benefactors and was to function as a part of the University of Minnesota Library system.

At its dedication on June 26, 1974, the library was home to approximately 90 periodicals, 200 current nursery and seed catalogs, and 3,000 volumes dealing with horticulture, natural history, and children's literature. By 2007 the library had 18,000 volumes, 350 periodicals, 1,400 current seed and nursery catalogues, as well as many titles in special collections. All are reference only. The entire collection ranges from magazines like *Ranger Rick* for young people to very specialized plant society bulletins, from light-hearted children's books to serious horticultural tomes.

On a visit to Washington, D.C., Eleanor Andersen had visited the Smithsonian's Renwick Gallery which was exhibiting some of the country's leading woodworkers.

There she saw and was impressed with the work of George Nakashima, and in a stroke of inspiration, the Andersens elected to commission him to create furnishings for the library.

Born in 1905, Nakashima was trained as an architect at the Massachusetts Institute of Technology and later studied woodworking. Nakashima was not simply a woodworker, however; he was a sensitive philosopher with deeply held beliefs. In speaking of his work, he wrote, "We work with boards from these trees, to fulfill their yearning for a second life, to release their richness

Andersen Library is a fine research facility for staff and visitors alike. Handsome furniture, designed and built by the well-known craftsman George Nakashima enhances this spectacular setting for the library's 18,000 volumes.

Some of the earliest volumes in the library's collections date from the sixteenth century.

Richard Isaacson has been librarian at the Andersen Horticultural Library since 1985. In 1992 he was awarded the Charles Robert Long Award of Merit by the Council on Botanical and Horticultural Libraries in recognition of his accomplishments at the Arboretum.

and beauty. From these plants, we fashion objects useful to man and if nature wills, things of beauty. In any case, these objects harmonize the rhythm of nature to fulfill the tree's destiny and ours."[12]

To design furniture for the library, Nakashima traveled to the Arboretum to study the space itself. From that visit he crafted tables, chairs, and display cases, principally of American black walnut. The low table is made from a burl of an English oak at least four hundred years old. All his pieces show respect for the trees from which they are fashioned and exhibit a graceful naturalness.

In 1988, a 6,500-square-foot addition was designed by architects Elden Morrison and Associates, giving the library a climate-controlled, secure space with compact shelving for its collection of historic materials which include nursery and seed catalogues and rare horticultural and botanical works.

In addition to its fine physical facilities, its furnishings and collections, the library is staffed with helpful, knowledgeable people who field queries of all kinds. June Rogier served as librarian until June of 1985. Richard Isaacson, who came from the Eleanor Squire Library at the Cleveland Botanic Garden, became librarian in December of that year and continues to the present time. In recognition of his accomplishments, Isaacson was awarded the 1992 Charles Robert Long Award of Merit by the Council on Botanical and Horticultural Libraries (CBHL)—an honor given infrequently and at the discretion of a CBHL committee. In his book, *A Man's Reach,* Elmer Andersen said of him, "Isaacson has lifted the Andersen

Library to prominence in the horticulture field."[13]

The library is open seven days a week to help visitors and callers answer plant questions. In 2005, the library received approximately eleven thousand reference inquiries dealing with topics such as design, pest control, and plant suppliers. Gardeners come in looking for information on herb use or suggestions as to which plants to grow in the shade. Some arrive carrying bugs or branches for identification. Whatever the query, the library staff is ready and willing to make sure the answer is found.

With the publication funds provided by Elmer and Eleanor Andersen, the library has published books on horticulture, landscape design, and the natural world. These include titles by naturalist Jim Gilbert, landscape architect Marion Fry, and former Arboretum director Leon C. Snyder.

The most widely used publication is the *Andersen Horticultural Library's Source List of Plants and Seeds*, first published in 1987. In 2004 the sixth edition was issued, and the *Source List* was also made available online where, entitled *Plant Information Online* (plantinfo.umn.edu), it also hosts a large citation index and a guide to North American nurseries. Both the published and online versions have been favorably reviewed by experts and praised by users. In 1999 the *Source List* won an American Association of Botanic Gardens and Arboreta award for program excellence, a recognition given to the best public garden program in North America.

In addition to the *Source List*, researchers can use *FPI:*

Flowering Plant Index on *Plant Information Online*. *FPI* is used throughout the world to find illustrations and information on many of the world's flowering plants. The *Index* provides full family, genus, species, and subspecies level of plant names on one million entries.

The library has been imaginative and forward-thinking in its Special Collection acquisitions. A tour through its exceptional holdings is a virtual trip through the last six centuries of horticulture and related disciplines. Here one can see examples of seed catalogues, hand-colored plates from the eighteenth and nineteenth centuries, herbals from the 1500s, Victorian gardening magazines, and early records of Minnesota's flora.

From the beginning Elmer Andersen encouraged the library to excel in a particular area, and it was June Rogier who discovered that niche. Through her work with the Council on Botanical and Horticultural Libraries (CBHL), Rogier came to realize the importance of historic seed and nursery catalogs as well as the lack of attention the collecting of these catalogues was being given by libraries nationwide. One of the most heavily used research collections, these historic catalogs are a resource for people interested in the history of plants, in botanical illustrations, in economic and cultural history, and in the history of nursery and seed companies. Not only useful for their information, they are often filled with splendid illustrations of plants and gardens.

Since 1980, the staff members have made a concerted effort to acquire these catalogs, and through their efforts, the AHL now has one of the most significant collections in North America including fifty thousand historic catalogs, some dating from the 1830s and many of which are quite rare.

In January 1988, the Friends of the Andersen Horticultural Library was organized. The initial meeting attracted thirty-two people eager to help design and promote the projects of Andersen Library, and from that first small band, the group has grown to around sixty members who meet quarterly and publish an attractive newsletter twice yearly.

The goals of the Friends are to serve as an advisory group to the library, to stimulate public awareness, and to help with financial support. Their main fund raiser, the October book sale, raises around $10,000 annually, and these funds have made it possible for the library to purchase a security system, compact shelving, and computers, and to support an endowment for the acquisition of exceptional books.

VOLUNTEERS

From their beginnings, the Arboretum and the Research Center have been fortunate to receive enormous support from hundreds of dedicated volunteers. As the facilities have grown, so has the cadre of individuals willing to donate their time and energy in support of the institution. By 2006, the Volunteer Program Coordinator, Liz Nystrom, was supervising the efforts of eight hundred volunteers, all busy with activities ranging from stuffing envelopes to studying how a maple tree produces sap. The state of Minnesota estimates that each volunteer hour is worth $18.50 to an institution, and at that rate, the thirty-five thousand hours contributed in 2006 represented a value of $647,000.

Nystrom has divided the service areas into six main categories: gardening crew, clerical, events/exhibits, the auxiliary, education/interpretation (tour guides, adult education, and work at the Learning Center), and special assignments. In the latter category, an individual works one-on-one with a staff member on a specific job. Volunteers are placed according to their interests and abilities, and the staff's needs. Training is based on the work assignment. Tour guides receive on-going instruction in classes taught by

The First Volunteer

Merv Eisel, an original member of the Arboretum staff, told the story of the first Arboretum volunteer in the 1980 Annual Report:

". . . it was in 1964 that we had our first volunteer working in the arboretum. While I was foreman, a woman searching for the maintenance crew found me on the then mostly undeveloped grounds. She said that she was interested in working in the arboretum. I apologetically told her that we could only hire students. Her response was enthusiastic, 'Oh, I don't want to be *paid*, I just want to work here.' That woman was Marion Cooper, who was then an apartment dweller after many years of enjoying her own garden. Over the years she did many tasks at the arboretum. She weeded, removed spent flowers, picked up branches and twigs on the trails, and served as a receptionist on weekends. There were many times that she worked more than 40 hours a week."[14]

Shirley Mah Kooyman and Sandy Tanck. In addition to the inherent satisfactions of volunteering, workers receive recognition at yearly events: a gala appreciation dinner in the spring and a barbecue/potluck in the fall.

Nystrom has noted several characteristics of the Arboretum's volunteers. First, they come to the facility on their own rather than being recruited (recruitment being unnecessary because so many offer their help without solicitation). Second, they love to learn, and Nystrom says that the educational component of volunteering is a significant attraction the Arboretum has to offer that is not always available in other volunteer milieus. "No matter what area they work in," she said, "volunteers will learn about plants and gardening. And they pick more up the longer they stay."[15]

Indeed, volunteers work in every area of HRC and Arboretum functions. Skilled carpenters have built birdhouses and fences; retired scientists have assisted in developing better plants for the northern climate; architects have donated building plans; writers have contributed to the newsletter.

Lastly, Nystrom notes, Arboretum volunteers are typically very loyal, working for years at the facility. "A number have been here twenty to twenty-five years," she stated. "They become so dedicated, especially when they form an attachment to someone on the staff, such as the head of a gardening crew. That loyalty gives them a breadth of knowledge which is very valuable to our institution."[16]

Loyal volunteers are the backbone of the Arboretum and the Horticultural Research Center. They contribute hundreds of hours weekly in office and garden duties, and often remain volunteers for years.

From the earliest days of the Arboretum, volunteers have stepped forward to fill the Arboretum's needs working as tour guides, gardeners, ticket collectors, and fund raisers. In the summer of 1968, members of the group, then called Volunteer Guides, met to organize an official volunteer organization.

The group's leaders that day included Edith Herman (President of the Guides), Georgia Bachman, Marianne Allen, Marion Cooper, Anne Neils (Doerr) and others. They took the name Landscape Arboretum Auxiliary and adopted the goals of raising funds, promoting the Arboretum, guiding tours, serving as weekend greeters, and sponsoring special events such as the Autumn Festival.

This energetic and generous group of women has expanded its mission and slate of activities in the forty years of its existence, adding a few men along the way. The members hold quarterly luncheon meetings, volunteer at staff-planned events, and sponsor five major fund-raising activities annually. For years interested members have gathered in Frog Hollow, once a machine shed and then an education center, located just off Three-Mile Drive, to create arrangements of dried plant material to be sold at the Fall Festival and the

The Fall Festival, a gala sale of crafts connected with gardens and gardening, was a long-running event at the Arboretum. The women are (left to right) Florence Johnstone, her sister-in-law Inky Johnstone, and Shirley Engh.

December Holiday Open House. From the dried plants they fashion swags, centerpieces, topiaries, wreaths, candle holders, and a myriad of other items.

The Spring Plant sale, held in May, is always enticing to area gardeners in search of hard-to-find plants. The annual summer Garden Tour, held over three days, attracts hundreds of people who view private area gardens and lunch on the Morgan Terrace. The Fall Festival, which ran from 1968 to 2005, was a perennial favorite. From its beginning, the Festival drew thousands of visitors who participated in activities and shopped for dried flower arrangements and other items crafted from plants by the Auxiliary. The fall arrangements are still sold one weekend during the autumn activity programs. The year is capped off with a Holiday Sale featuring such items as hand-made wreaths, ornaments, and decorations.

The combined fund-raising events bring in thousands of dollars a year which the Auxiliary returns to programs and equipment for the Arboretum. Not only a major contributor to the Arboretum grounds and gardens, operations, and programs, in recent years the Auxiliary has also supported the Therapeutic Horticulture Programs, the Urban Garden Programs, the repair of the Ordway Picnic Shelter, and the restoration of the Berens family cabin, turning it into the Arboretum's History Center.

On the occasion of the Auxiliary's twenty-fifth anniversary, Arboretum director, Peter Olin, commented, "When one looks at the development and growth of the Arboretum over the past twenty-four years, it is dif-

ficult to imagine what we would be if the Auxiliary had not been there to help. They have been the backbone and the flesh, the mentor and the student, the laborer and the luster. Even more difficult, imagine what the Arboretum's future would be without the Auxiliary here as safety-net, helper, and friend."[17]

THE MINNESOTA LANDSCAPE ARBORETUM FOUNDATION

In 1970 the Minnesota Landscape Arboretum Foundation was established. The first year there were nine trustees including John E. P. Morgan, Vincent K. Bailey, Archibald B. Jackson, Cecil March, Hugh G. S. Peacock, Robert J. Odegard, H. J. Sloan, Phillip H. Smith, and Leon C. Snyder. This Board quickly became an important advisory and fund-raising group for the Arboretum.

Over time the group grew in size and complexity until in 1981, the Foundation Board established a new official category of membership, that of honorary trustee. First to be elected to that position were Sam Morgan and Cliff Sommer, both long-time Arboretum supporters and policy makers. By 2008 the maximum number of trustees was capped at thirty-six, though the number of honorary trustees kept growing. Over the years the Foundation has spearheaded numerous financial campaigns, assisted in developing policy, and advised on matters of architecture, grounds, and community awareness. Within the larger group, there are several committees which focus on specific topics: development, finance, education, and nominating.

In the 1992 Annual Report, then President Helen Hartfiel noted that "the principal purpose of the Board of Directors is to solicit and manage gifts of money and

In 2003 this praying mantis was one of thirteen "Big Bugs" in the Arboretum's first major summer exhibition.

of 1998-2003, of which the Arboretum was a part, $65.5 million was raised, the largest amount in its history, and the Foundation's fund-raising leaders made this possible.

Reflecting on the Foundation's influence, Arboretum Director Peter Olin, stated:

Since its inception, the Minnesota Landscape Arboretum Foundation has been the main generator of funds for high quality maintenance. This has created one of our hallmarks, beautifully maintained gardens and collections. It has allowed our educational outreach programs to grow dramatically while remaining relevant. Further, the Foundation has been the source of funds generated for nearly all capital construction including many buildings, most collections, and all gardens and exhibits. Without the Foundation, the Arboretum would never have attained its present place as one of Minnesota's treasures.[19]

property so that [the Arboretum's] goals come to fruition."[18] That year the Board raised $1.04 million to fund the operating budget and increased the endowment to over $3.6 million. The Board's goal, as noted in 1992, remains the Foundation's primary mission. To that end, the Foundation has contributed generously each year to the Arboretum's needs, making possible new buildings, programs, staffing, and grounds improvements. By 2008 those contributions constituted 40 percent of the Arboretum's operating budget.

During the University of Minnesota's capital campaign

From a dream in the mind of a few individuals, the Arboretum has grown to become a year-round attraction for thousands of people, with hundreds more, amateurs and professionals, involved as staff and volunteers. The original 160 acres purchased from Dr. Berens in 1958 has burgeoned into a destination with interests for many, as not only numerous stunning gardens and walks, but also workshops, classes and events await the visitor. Within its 1,047 current acres, from early spring with its delicate wildflowers through the bitterest winter with its snowcapped trails and trees, the Arboretum has beauties to delight all ages. From its humble beginnings, it has truly become a northern treasure.

Andersen Library Publications

Fry, Marion M. *A Space of One's Own: the Lively Process of Personal Landscape Design,* 1992.

Gilbert, James R. *Jim Gilbert's Nature Notebook: a Daily Guide to Many Biological and Physical Events in Nature in the Upper Midwest, Using the Minnesota Landscape Arboretum as the Vantage Point,* 1983.

Gilbert, James R. *Through Minnesota's Seasons with Jim Gilbert,* 1987.

Isaacson, Richard T. *Andersen Horticultural Library's Source List of Plants and Seeds.* 1st ed., 1987; 2nd ed., 1989; 3rd ed., 1993; 4th ed., 1996; 5th ed., 2000; 6th ed., 2004.

Isaacson, Richard T. *FPI: Flowering Plant Index,* 1991- (Online).

Plant Information Online, 1998.

Snyder, Leon C. *Native Plants for Northern Gardens,* 1991.

Snyder, Leon C. *Trees and Shrubs for Northern Gardens,* 1980; Rev. ed., 2000.

NOTES

CHAPTER TWO

1. Franklin Curtiss-Wedge, *The History of Freeborn County* (Chicago: H.C. Cooper, Jr. & Co., 1912), p. 238.
2. A. E. Hutchins, "Historical Notes," *Minnesota Horticulturist* (June 1966), p. 73.
3. U. P. Hedrick, *History of Horticulture in America to 1860* (Portland, Oregon: Timber Press, 1988), p. 451.
4. A. W. Latham, "The Proposed Fruit-Breeding Experiment Station," *Minnesota Horticulturist*, v. 35, no. 2 (February 1907), p. 65.
5. *Ibid.*
6. Charles Haralson, "How Members May Assist the State Fruit Breeding Farm," *Minnesota Horticulturist*, v. 36, no. 11 (November 1908), p. 401.
7. Charles Haralson, "The State Fruit Breeding Farm in 1922," *Minnesota Horticulturist*, v. 51, no. 1 (January 1922), p. 34.
8. Charles Haralson, "Annual Examination of the Minnesota State Fruit Breeding Farm for 1916," *Minnesota Horticulturist*, v. 45, no. 1 (January 1917), p. 56.
9. *Ibid.*
10. F. E. Haralson, "Fruit Breeding Farm (A) General Report," *Minnesota Horticulturist*, v. 57, no. 1 (January 1929), p. 71.
11. *Ibid.*
12. W. H. Alderman and F. E. Haralson, "Minnesota Fruit Breeding Farm 1934," *Minnesota Horticulturist*, v. 63, no.1 (January 1935), p. 31.
13. W. H. Alderman and F. E. Haralson, "The Fruit Breeding Farm Report for 1936," *Minnesota Horticulturist*, v. 65, no. 1 (January 1937), p. 5.
14. Interview with Professor James Luby, June 2006.
15. *Ibid.*
16. "1954 Report of the Fruit Breeding Farm Visitors Committee," *Minnesota Horticulturist*, v. 82, no. 9 (October 1954), p. 143.
17. Interview with Peter Olin, June 2006.

CHAPTER THREE

1. Taped Interview of Leon C. Snyder, owned by Andersen Horticultural Library, Minnesota Landscape Arboretum.
2. *Ibid.*
3. *Ibid.*
4. *Ibid.*
5. *Ibid.*
6. *Ibid.*
7. *Ibid.*

8. Interview with Peter Olin, July 2005.
9. *Ibid.*
10. Merv Eisel, "Minnesota's Number One Horticulturist," *Minnesota Landscape Arboretum News*, v. 3, no. 3 (Fall 1983), p. 5.
11. Francis de Vos, "Looking Ahead," *Landscape Arboretum Annual Report* (1977), p. 6.

CHAPTER FOUR

1. Theodore Bost, *A Frontier Family in Minnesota, Letters of Theodore and Sophie Bost, 1851-1920* (Minneapolis: University of Minnesota Press, 1981), p. 89.
2. *Ibid.*, pp. 87-88.
3. Leon C. Snyder, "The Arboretum Site," *University of Minnesota Landscape Arboretum*, Miscellaneous Report 38 (April 1960), p. 4.
4. Interview with Peter Olin, June 2005.
5. *Ibid.*
6. Leon C. Snyder, "The Landscape Arboretum, a Report of Progress, 14th Year," *Minnesota Landscape Arboretum Annual Report* (1972), p. 3.
7. Leon C. Snyder, "The Landscape Arboretum, a Report of Progress, 16th Year," *Minnesota Landscape Arboretum Annual Report* (1974), p. 3.
8. Leon C. Snyder, "The Landscape Arboretum, a Report of Progress, 17th Year," *Minnesota Landscape Arboretum Annual Report* (1975), p. 3.
9. Francis de Vos, "Looking Ahead," *Minnesota Landscape Arboretum Annual Report* (1977), p. 6.
10. Francis de Vos, "Director's Message," *Minnesota Landscape Arboretum News*, v. 6, no. 2 (Summer 1986), p. 3.
11. Leon C. Snyder, "The Landscape Arboretum, a Report of Progress, 16th Year," *Minnesota Landscape Arboretum Annual Report* (1974), p. 3.
12. Julie Clausen, "Japanese Garden Will Grace the U—Despite the Elements," *Minnesota Daily* (October 2, 1984).
13. Francis de Vos, "Demonstration Gardens Bring Ideas Home," *Minnesota Landscape Arboretum News*, v. 6, no. 2 (Summer 1986), p. 1.
14. Interview with Peter Olin, July 2005.
15. Minnesota Landscape Arboretum Mission Statement, March 15, 1999.
16. Dave Stevenson, "The First Collections," *Minnesota Landscape Arboretum News*, v. 17, no. 1 (January-February 1998), p. 13.
17. Susan Galatowitsch, "Susan Galatowitsch, Recreating a Diverse Sedge

Meadow," *Water Laws, Water Resources Law, Policy and Commentary*, http://www.waterlaws.com/commentary/interviews/galatowitsch_interview.html.
18. Interview with Peter Olin, August 2005.

CHAPTER FIVE

1. "Objectives," *University of Minnesota Landscape Arboretum*, Miscellaneous Report 38 (April 1960), p. 4.
2. Sandy Tanck, "The Children's Garden," *Minnesota Landscape Arboretum Annual Report* (1980), p. 24.
3. "Arboretum Program Garners Top National Honors," *Minnesota Landscape Arboretum News*, v. 12, no. 3 (May-June 1993), p. 1.
4. Sandy Tanck, "Andrus Brings Enthusiasm to Job," *Minnesota Landscape Arboretum News*, v. 5, no. 1 (Spring 1985), p. 14.
5. Interview with Tim Kenny, June 2006.
6. Interview with Shirley Kooyman, August 2006.
7. Interview with Jeanne Larson, August 2006.
8. Maria Klein, "HRC Renovation Boosts Production, Prestige," *Minnesota Landscape Arboretum News*, v. 19, no. 6 (November-December 2000), p. 1.
9. "Apple Descriptions," *Sponsel's Minnesota Harvest* (2006), Online journal. http:www.minnesotaharvest.net/apple_crips.htm.
10. Interview with Dave Bedford, June 2006.
11. Sarah Barker, "Grape Expectations," *Minnesota Magazine,* v. 105, no. 4 (March-April 2006), p. 25.
12. June M. Rogier and Richard T. Isaacson, *Andersen Horticultural Library: the First 25 Years* (Chanhassen, Minnesota: Andersen Horticultural Library, 1996), p. 9.
13. Elmer L. Andersen, *A Man's Reach* (Minneapolis: University of Minnesota Press, 2000), p. 358.
14. Mervin C. Eisel, "Working Ambassadors: The Arboretum Volunteers," *Minnesota Landscape Arboretum Annual Report for 1980*, p. 27.
15. Interview with Liz Nystrom, October 2006.
16. *Ibid.*
17. Interview with Peter Olin, September 2006.
18. Helen C. Hartfiel, "President's Report," *Minnesota Landscape Arboretum News*, v. 11, no. 1 (January-February 1992), p. 3.
19. Interview with Peter Olin, July 2006.

ACKNOWLEDGMENTS

ANY UNDERTAKING of this size requires the help of numerous people. I was fortunate in writing *Northern Treasure* to have the help and expertise of many. There were those who helped me locate information and those who corrected the bits I had wrong. To them all I am extremely grateful.

My first thanks go to director Peter Olin, who believed in my ability to handle the project, answered endless questions, and explained the basic workings of the Arboretum. He read the draft several times, making corrections and additions as needed, and was constantly enthused about the project.

Second, I would like to thank Richard Isaacson, head librarian at the Andersen Horticultural Library, who opened the library to me, literally and figuratively. He and his staff became like a second family and welcomed me daily as I worked on the book. A quiet table there became my base of operations. Richard has an encyclopedic knowledge of plants and plant nomenclature. He kindly imparted to me again and again necessary information about the plants at the Arboretum. Richard read the manuscript twice, correcting any errors of commission or omission and selected the felicitous title, *Northern Treasure*, for our book. His staff, including Susan Cross, Renee Jensen, Susan Moe, and Christine Aho, explained the contents of various collections within the library as well as facets of Arboretum history.

Gardeners are a vital part of the Arboretum and Horticultural Research Center (HRC) structure. They design, plant, evaluate, and tend all areas of the grounds. Importantly for this project, they read the sections that pertained to their areas and provide much-needed feedback. I would especially like to mention Ted Pew, Richard Gjertson, Duane Otto, Julia Bohnen, and Ricky Garza.

Arboretum horticulturists and educators graciously granted interviews, explaining the histories of their departments and current projects. Their enthusiasm and dedication was contagious. Shirley Kooyman, Mary Meyer, Dave Bedford, Harold Pellett, Sandy Tanck, Jim Luby, Jean Larson, Pete Moe, Tim Kenny, Dave Stevenson, Liz Nystrom, and Jan Malysza all shared their knowledge and I thank them.

Perpetual volunteer and walking Arboretum encyclopedia, Helen King, took me under her wing at the outset. She introduced me to folks in every area and encouraged me when I was despairing. By welcoming me to the morning coffee table, she made a place for me to meet the gardeners on an informal basis. In the process she became my friend.

With his stunning photographs, John Gregor translated visually the beauty of the Arboretum and Research Center, giving life to my text. His photographs have insured that folks will remember this book. Mary Susan Oleson's design for the book provides an ideal showcase for John's photographs.

Others outside the Arboretum and Research Center lent generous support. Dave Hanson, at the University of Minnesota, spent a day reviewing archival photographs with me. He made available for our use significant early shots of the HRC and the Arboretum. Editor Marcia Aubineau perfected the final manuscript. Beth Williams at Afton Press helped me sift through hundreds of photographs, organized them, and provided production assistance at every phase of this book project. And a final thanks to Patricia McDonald at Afton Press, who did her usual fine job of pulling together all the pieces into a beautiful whole.

SUSAN DAVIS PRICE

Alderman, W. H., 32–34, **35**
Alkire, Darrel, 57
Alkire Drive, 14, 57, 96
Allen, Marianne, 130
American Academy of Neurology, 84
American Association of Botanic Gardens
    and Arboreta, 52, 109; award, 127
American Horticultural Society, 51–52
American Horticulture Therapy Association, 116
Andersen, Eleanor J., 124–125, 127
Andersen, Elmer L., **107**, 124, 126–127
Andersen Horticultural Library. *See* Elmer L.
    and Eleanor J. Andersen Horticultural Library
Andrus, John III, and Marion, 49, 109. *See also*
    Marion Andrus Learning Center and the Sally
    Pegues Oswald Growing Place for Kids
Anne Barber Dunlap Walkway, 79
Anne Doerr Memorial Grove, 90
Anne M. Koempel Clematis Collection, 80
Apple House, 21–22, **22**
Autumn (or Fall) Festival, 22–23, 130–131, **130**

Bachman, Georgia, 130
Bachman, Lee W., 71
Bailey, Gordon S. Sr., 91. *See also* Gordon S.
    Bailey Shrub Walk
Bailey, Vincent K., 131
Baldwin, Herb, 78, 82
Bartz, Dr. Jim, 119
Bedford, Dave, 120–123, **120**
Behrens, Dr. Richard and Anne 73
Behrens Weed Exhibit, 73
Bennett/Johnson Prairie, 17, **19**, 85–88, **87**, **89**
Bennett, Mr. and Mrs. Russell, 46, 87
Berens Cabin, 23, **42**, 50, 131
Berens, Dr. Herbert J., 43, 132
    property of, 44–46
Berens Woods, 26
Berry, Scott, 48
Better World Report, 2006, 121
Blackbourn, A. R., 92
Blackman, Anne Hueg, 98
Blong, Theodore and Doris, 79
Blong Walkway, 79
Bohnen, Julia, 100
Bonestroo, Rosene, Anderlik and Associates, 102-103
Bost, Theodore, 57
Brinda, Tom, 64
Brooks, Conley and Marney, 49
Burdick Craddick Lott Walkway, 79, **80**
Burke Griggs Annual Garden, 17, 73–74, **74**
Burrell, Colston, 67, 113
Buss, Sheri, 102

Capen, Joan and Gary, 86
Capen Prairie Garden, 85–86, **87**
Carlson, Bryan, 48
Carver County Mounted Posse, 23
Chicago Botanic Garden, 52, 113
Children's Garden(s), 18, 105, 107, 110–111
Children's Harvest Fair, 20
CityFresh, 110–111
Cloistered Garden, 66–67
Clotilde Irvine Sensory Garden, 53, 82, **85**, **115**, 116
Cooper, Marion, 128, 130

Crabapple Collection, 79, 88, **97**
Cross Cutting Garden, 71
Cross, Marion, 71

Dahlberg, Kenneth and Betty Jayne, 58
Dahlberg Welcoming Terrace, 58
Damon Farber and Associates, 80
Dayton, Grace B., 43. *See also* Grace B. Dayton
    Wildflower Garden
    and sons, 81-82
Dayton, Mary Lee and Wallace, 100
Deats, Dr. Edith Potter, 93
Depression era, effect on fruit farm, 33, 123
de Vos, Francis, 52–53, **52**, 55, 62, 68, 77, 79, 107.
    See also Francis de Vos Home Demonstration
    Garden
Dodge, Olivia Irvine, 85
Doerr, Anne Neils, 130
Downing, Edna, 73
Driscoll, Mr. and Mrs. W. John, 64
Dunlap, Anne Barber, 79
Dyers' Garden, 66–68

Easley, Dennis, 82
Edmundson Garden for Outdoor Living, 70
Edmundson, Dr. Hugh and Joyce, 70
Edna Downing Seasonal Display, 73
Eisel, Merv, 39, 51-52, 54, 106, **108**, 128
Elden Morrison and Associates, 126
Eleanor Lawler Pillsbury Shade Tree Exhibit, 53, 85, **86**
Elmer L. and Eleanor J. Andersen Horticultural
    Library, 25–26, 53, 124–128, **125**, **126**
    assistance for gardeners, 26
    Friends of, 25, 128
    publications, 127, 135
    Used Book Sale, 55
Elizabeth Carr Slade Perennial Garden, 17, **24**, 53,
    62–64, **65**, 66, 74
Ellerbe Becket, 48
Environmental Planning and Design, 64, 68, 77
Erickson, Marilyn, 109

Fallon, Dr. Virgil, 74
Fink, Daniel, 30
Flack, Archie, 43
Fragrant Herb Garden, 18, **18**, 66-67
Francis de Vos Home Demonstration Garden, 53, 68, **69**
Freeman, Douglas O., 78
Frerichs, Johanna, 88. *See also* Johanna Frerichs
    Garden for Wildlife
Frog Hollow, 22, 130
Frost, William, 92. *See also* Maze Garden
Fruit and Vegetable Garden, 69, **70**, **71**
Fruit Breeding Farm, **28**, 30–34, **31- 35**, 37–39, 43,
    45, 50, 79, 96, 116, 118.
    See also Minnetonka Fruit Farm
    See also National Fruit Breeding Program
Fry, Marion, 127

Galatowitsch, Susan, 100, 102
Gallistel, Audrey and Albert, 100
Gallistel Overlook, 21, 100
Garden for a Family of Four, 69
Garden for Small Spaces, 71, **73**
Garden Writers of America, 54

Gardner, Dr. Gary, 119
Gideon, Peter Miller, 29–30, **29**, 45
Gilbert, Cass, 46
Gilbert, James R. (Jim), 127
Gjertson, Richard, 82, 88
Gordon S. Bailey Shrub Walk, 53, 79, 90–91, **91**
Grace B. Dayton Wildflower Garden, 14, 23, **23**, 79,
    81–82, **83**, **84**
Granlund, Paul, sculpture, **27**
Greeley, Horace, 29
Green Heron Pond, 14, **25**, 61–62
Griggs, Mary Livingston, and Mary Griggs Burke
    Foundation, 75

Haggerty, Ruth and Dan, 79
Hagstrom, Jim, 60-61, 85
Haralson, Charles, 31–33, **32**, 79
Haralson, Fred, 32, 33, 34, **34**, 79
Hare & Hare, 45
Harris, John, 29
Hartfiel, Helen, 49, 131
Hartfiel, William, 49
Hebeisin, Robert and Sally, 49
Heger, Mike, 64
Hella and Bill Hueg Lilac Collection, **16**, 96, **99**
Hemstad, Peter, 123–24
Herb Overlook (or Wedding Tower), 66
Herman, Edith, 130
Hermann Farm, 46
Highpoint Endowment Circle, 90
Hill Family Foundation, 44
Hodgman, Elizabeth and Charles, 84
Hoeft, Leonard and Mary Lou, 95
Hokanson, Stan, 124
Hoover, Emily, 105
Horticultural Research Center, 16, 21, 25, 36–37, 39,
    46, 54, 96, 116, 118–119, **118**, **122**, 123, **129**, 138
Howard, Charles, family, 78
Howard Fern Walk, 78
Hueg, Hella and Bill, 96. *See also* Hella and Bill
    Hueg Lilac Collection
Huff, Rusty, 84
Hugelin, Eldon M., 50
Hultgren-Haralson Walk, 79

ice cream social, 21, 55
International Congress on Education, 116
Iris Pond, **2**, 17
Isaacson, Richard, 126-127, **126**

Jackson, Archibald B., 131
Japanese Garden, 26, 53
Jeffers, Herm, 66
Johanna Frerichs Garden for Wildlife, 79, 88, **90**, 91
Johnson, Albert G., 39, 87-88

Kathleen Wright Garden, 58, **59**
Kawana, Koichi, 75. *See also* Seisui-Tei
Kazakhstan orchards, 37, 39
Keating Greenhouse, 69, 113
Keating, Stephen F. and Mary, 69
Kenny, Tim, 110–111
Kenwood Garden Club, 92
King, Helen, 23
Kitchen Herb Garden, 66, **67**

Knot Garden, 66–67, **68**
Knutson, Bruce, 49
Knutson, Donald T., family, 49, 109
Kooyman, Shirley Mah, 112–113, 129

Lake Minnetonka Garden Club, 44
Lang, Helen, Charitable Trust, 79
Lang, Theodora, 79
Lang Peony Walk, **20**, 78
Larson, Jean, 113, **114**, 115–116
Larson, John, 49
Legeros, Nick, 92
Leicester, Andrew, 66
Leon C. Snyder Education and Research Building, 47, **47**, **48**, **51**, 60, 65, 74, 77, 79, 107
Lightly, Richard W., 109
Linden Collection, **4**, **97**
Lindquist, Merieda and Arthur, 79
Lindquist, Russell and Avis, 79
Lindquist Walk, 79
Luby, James, 36, 37, 119, 121, 123
Ludwick Naturalistic Garden, 68, **69**
Ludwick, William F. and Harriet, 68
Lundie, Edwin, 44, 46–47, 57, 80, 92, 107, **107**
Lyman, Mrs. Frederick C. (Clara Cross), 44

MacMillan Auditorium, 49
MacMillan, Mrs. Cargill (Pauline Whitney), 44, 77
    See also Pauline Whitney MacMillan Hosta Glade
MacMillan, Sarah Stevens, 60. See also Sarah
    Stevens MacMillan Terrace Garden
Mansfield, Anna Katharine, 123
March, Cecil, 131
Margaret and Harley Gronseth Herb Garden, 66, 70, **72**
Margaret Rivers Fund of Stillwater, 61–62
Marilyn Nafstad Addition (to Palma J. Wilson
    Rose Garden), 80, **81**
Marion Andrus Learning Center and the Sally
    Pegues Oswald Growing Place for Kids,
    49, **50**, 53, 103, 105, 110
Marshall, Missy, 64, 66
Marshall Tyler Rausch, 66
Maze Garden, 79, 92, **94**
McFadden, Katherine, 113
McKinnon, Jane, 107
McNamara, Steve, 40
McQuinn Great Hall, 49
McReynolds, Isaac W., 29
Men's Garden Club of Minneapolis, 43, 50
Men's Garden Club of America, 51
Metropolitan Council, 103
Meyer, Dr. Mary Hockenberry, 98, 115
Meyer-Deats Conservatory, 93, **95**
Minnehaha Creek Watershed District, 103
Minnesota Grape Growers Association, 123
Minnesota Herb Society, 66
Minnesota Horticulturist, 30, 34
Minnesota Landscape Arboretum
    Collections, 95–100
    educational programs, 105–113, **112**, **114**
    map of, 96
    parking lot solutions 102–103, **103**
    publications, 127, 135
    themed exhibitions, 20–21
    travel tours, 54, 113
Minnesota Landscape Arboretum Auxiliary, 16,
    50, 54–55, 85, 107, 130–131
Minnesota Landscape Arboretum Foundation, 52,
    60, 131-132
Minnesota Landscape Arboretum News, 54
Minnesota Nursery and Landscape Association, 91
Minnesota Rose Society, 15, 79–81

Minnesota State Horticultural Society, 30, 32, 38,
    43–44, 112, 116
Minnetonka Fruit Farm, 30
Moe, Peter, 23
Morgan, John E. P., 47–48, **107**, 131
Morgan, Sam, 131
Morgan Terrace, 61, 131

Nakashima, George, 125–126
Nash, Katherine, 78
National Fruit Breeding Program, 33, 36, 119
Neilson Foundation, 49
Nelson, Thomas and Jane, 92
Newton Dining Terrace, 58, **58**
Newton, Patricia A., 58
Norby, Kevin, 69
North Star Walking Trail, 26
Nystrom, Liz, 128–129

Odegard, Robert J., 131
Oertel Architects, 49
Olin, Peter, 40, 48, 53–55, **53**, 79, 60–61, 84, 98,
    102, 119, 112–113, 131–132
Ordway, Charlotte, 46
Ordway, John and Margaret, 75
Ordway Picnic Shelter, 22, 46, 107, **107**, 131
Ornamental Grasses, 79, 98, **99**, 119
Oswald, Charles W., 48, 49, 100
Oswald Visitor Center, **20**, 26, 46, 48-49, **48-49**,
    54, 57–58, **59**, 74
Otto, Duane, 17, 60, 64, 74

Palma J. Wilson Rose Garden, 15, **17**, 21, 46, 53,
    73–74, 79–81, **81**
Path Garden Club, 66
Patio and Container Garden, 72
Pauline Whitney MacMillan Hosta Glade, 18, 76–
    77, **77**, **133**
Paulson, Ruth and David, 55
Peacock, Hugh G. S., 131
Pellett, Harold, 39–40, **40**, 106, 124, 138
Pennock, Jevne, 79
Peterson, Andrew, 29
Pew, Ted, 69, 81
Phelps, Edmund, 96
Pierquet, Patrick, 37
Pillsbury, Mrs. John Sr. (Eleanor Lawler), 44, 85.
    See also Eleanor Lawler Pillsbury Shade Tree
    Exhibit
Pitz, Marjorie, 85
Plantmobile, 105, 109
Pond, Reverend G. H., 29
Price, Michael, 69

Rafferty Rafferty Tollefson Architects, 48
Rausch, Geoff, 64, 66, 68, 77, 79
Red Barn, **38**
Reedy Gallery, 49
Richard and Judith Spiegel Entry Garden, 17, 53, 60
Robin, Jim, 90, 92, 96, 103
Rock Garden, **13**, 15, 72–73, 84, **85**
Rock Garden Society of Minnesota, 72
Rogier, June, 124, 126, 127
Roller, Adele, 84
Rozumalski, Fred, 100, 102

Saint Paul Garden Club, 46, 52, 77
SALA Architects, 48. See also Oswald Visitor Center
Sally Pegues Oswald Growing Place for Kids, 49,
    50, 105, 110
Sarah Stevens MacMillan Terrace Garden, 17,
    53, 60–61, **61**

Schuth, Matt, **106**
Secret Gardens, **20**, 21, **55**
Seisui-Tei (or Garden of Pure Water), 26, 75, **76**
Sensory Wall Garden, 84
Shrub Rose Garden, 79, 91–92, **93**
Simonds, John, 52
Slawson, David, 75
Sloan, H. J., 131
Smith, Phillip H., 131
Snyder, Dr. Leon C., 34, **36**, 37–39, 43–46, 50–52, **51**,
    54, 57, 62, 73, 80–81, 92, 107, **107**, 124, 127, 131
Snyder, Leon C. Jr., 61–62, 96. See also Waterfall
    Garden
Snyder, Vera, 51
Sommer, Cliff, 131
Spiegel, Dick and Judith, 60
Spring Peeper Meadow, 21, 53, 98, 100, **101**, 102
Spring Plant Sale, 16, 54–55
Staples, Frederick B. Jr., 78
Staples Lilac Walk, 15, 78
Staples, Loring, 67, 78
Staples, Mary Cushman Wells, 67
Staples, Mary Peavey Wells, 78
Stephen F. Keating Terrace, 60
Stevenson, Dave, 95–96
Stushnoff, Dr. Cecil, 37
Sugarbush Pancake Brunch, 13
Sweatt Entry Terrace Garden, 58
Sweatt, Margaret L., and family, 58
Swenson, Elmer, 37

Tallinn Botanic Garden, 54
Tanck, Sandy, 107, 109, 129
Therapeutic Horticulture, 53, 82, 84, 113–116, 131
Three-Mile Drive, 23, 25, **44**, 55, 74, 79, 95–96,
    124, 130
Trumpet Creeper Tram, 23,55, 113
Twin City Herb Society, 66

United States National Arboretum, 52
University of Minnesota, 30–32, 37–39, 116, 117,
    121, 123, 124, 132

van Valkenburgh, Michael, 92
volunteers, 13, 16, 18, 22, 23, 25, 50, 51, 55, 58,
    60, 66, 87, 100, 106, 113, 124, 128, 129, **129**, 130

Warner, Barry, 102
Waterfall Garden, 61–62, **63**
Wedding Tower (or Herb Overlook), 66–67
Weeks, Steven, 85
Weir, T. H., 32, **36**
Wickman, Todd, 74
Williams Farm, **38**, 46
Wilson, Dr. John, 80. See also Palma J. Wilson
    Rose Garden
Winton, Mrs. David (Katherine Decker), 46, 79, 87
Winton Walkway, 79, **97**
Woodland Azalea Garden, 53, 77–78, **78**
Woody Landscape Plant Breeding Program, 38,
    39, **40**, 117–118, 124
Wright, Kathleen Mary, 58. See also Kathleen
    Wright Garden

Zins, Mike, 107
Zuzek, Kathy, 40

This book was designed
with care by

Mary Susan Oleson
NASHVILLE, TENNESSEE